The PLUMPJACK
Cookbook

The **PLUMPJACK** Cookbook

Great Meals for Good Living

Jeff Morgan

Foreword by Gavin Newsom

Food photography by Leigh Beisch

RODALE

Rodale books may be purchased for business or promotional use or for special sales.
For information, please write to:
Special Markets Department, Rodale Inc., 733 Third Avenue, New York, NY 10017

Printed in the United States of America
Rodale Inc. makes every effort to use acid-free ∞, recycled paper ♻.

Book design by Carol Angstadt
Food photographs by Leigh Beisch
Other photographs: pages vi, 1, 7, 12, 14–15, 21, 117, and 150–151 by Art Streiber; pages viii, 16, 23, 26–27,
and 180–181 by Steven Rothfeld; pages x and 134 by Angie Silvy; pages 2 and 3 by John Vaughan; page 4
by Skip Lovelady; page 9 by Russell Abraham; page 11 by John Clausen, © John Vaughan & Associates;
pages 36 and 66–67 by Art Gray; page 75 by Ed Anderson; and pages 112–113 by Katie Snider

Library of Congress Cataloging-in-Publication Data

Morgan, Jeff.
    The PlumpJack cookbook : great meals for good living / Jeff Morgan ; foreword by Gavin Newsom.
        p.   cm.
    Includes index.
    ISBN-13 978–1–59486–321–9   hardcover
    ISBN-10 1–59486–321–0   hardcover
        1. Cookery, American—California style.   2. Cookery—California   3. Cookery (Wine)
    4. PlumpJack Group.   I. Title.
    TX715.2.C34M67   2006
    641.5'9794—dc22   2006016281

Distributed to the book trade by Holtzbrinck Publishers

2   4   6   8   10   9   7   5   3   1   hardcover

We inspire and enable people to improve their lives and the world around them
For more of our products visit rodalestore.com or call 800-848-4735

To those chefs and winemakers

who transform eating and drinking

into an artistic pursuit

CONTENTS

Acknowledgments

Writing a book such as this one requires a lot of help from many individuals. First and foremost, the PlumpJack team of Rob Goldberg, Amanda Botelho, Hilary Newsom, and Rebecca Walder provided me with amazing "insider's" access and support. Pat Kelley gave me first-hand perspective on the founding of PlumpJack. And of course, PlumpJack chefs present and past generously shared their knowledge and recipes. They included: Larry Dunning, Kimball Jones, Mitchell Kaldrovich, Jonnatan Leiva, Jose Lemus, Alex Olson, James Ormsby, Wesley Shaw, and Jeff Smock.

PlumpJack founder Gavin Newsom, peripatetic and busy with his "day job" as mayor of San Francisco, was also amazingly generous with his limited free time.

None of this could have happened were it not for my friend and literary agent, Carole Bidnick, who understands the essence of publishing and how to connect the points with the dots. I must also express much gratitude to my editors—Miriam Backes, Roy Finamore, and Jennifer DeFilippi—and art director Carol Angstadt for their ongoing astute observations and for regularly sending me back to the drawing board in the interest of quality and clarity.

Additionally, it is a gift to have friends and neighbors who happen to be fabulous chefs as well. I regularly called on Lars Kronmark, at the Culinary Institute of America, and Todd Humphries, at Martini House, for the skinny on questions that posed particular challenge.

Then there were the tasters who never hesitated to eat—and critique—when the opportunity arose. Thank you, Chelsea Tipp, Michaela Barnett, Neidy Godinez, Steve Goldfinger, Nancy and Gary Brandl, the Judge and his bride, and John and Ann-Marie Conover. Thanks also to PlumpJack winemaker Tony Biagi, and to Daniel Moore, my partner in SoloRosa. Dan's attention to detail on the wine front gave me the freedom to focus on the food front when necessary.

A book about food, wine, and beautiful places needs illustration. From a visual angle, Russell Abraham, Ed Anderson, Leigh Beisch, John Clausen, Art Gray, Skip Lovelady, Steven Rothfeld, Angie Silvy, Katie Snider, Art Streiber, and John Vaughan provided a stunning backdrop for our message.

Finally, I don't know how my wife, Jodie, and my daughters, Skye and Zoe, put up with me during the arduous process of writing a book. They are constantly supportive and always loving. That's the greatest gift of all.

Jeff Morgan
St. Helena, Napa Valley

FOREWORD

PlumpJack founder
Gavin Newsom
on Fillmore Street,
where it all began

It's no accident we call ourselves "PlumpJack." This was Queen Elizabeth's nickname for Jack Falstaff, who appeared in four of her favorite William Shakespeare plays. The fun-loving Falstaff was audacious and irreverent and always ready for a good meal. I like to think that we—along with those who visit our restaurants, hotels, wine shops, and Napa Valley winery—share a similar perspective.

At each PlumpJack location, we strive to create an ambience that captures a distinctive flavor and character. For us, living well is about something more than fine dining and elegant accommodations. It also means respecting the earth and leaving a legacy for future generations. The PlumpJack restaurants and hotels are set in some of the most breathtaking landscapes in Northern California. And we want to keep them that way. That's why sustainable farming methods are in place at our vineyards, and locally grown produce is brought to the dinner table at each of our restaurants. Clearly, we have the good fortune to live and work between the earth and the stars. It's a privilege we need to honor.

I believe a top-notch dining experience should also be an accessible one. We seek elegance without pretense in every PlumpJack restaurant. To this end, we offer wines for only a small fraction above their retail value. In the early days, this caused an uproar among certain restaurateurs who charged double our prices. They protested loudly and were joined by a number of wineries that refused to sell us their wines. But we thought everyone should be able to enjoy good wine with a good meal. We wanted to preserve a time-honored tradition that had become too exclusive for too many of us. With time, many of our restaurateur colleagues have come to share our philosophy. As a result, diners throughout the San Francisco Bay area and beyond are now enjoying progressively priced wine lists. And our winery friends who originally jumped ship have all returned.

I must admit we enjoy turning tradition on its head. That's why we put a screw cap on our most expensive Cabernet Sauvignon. A lot of people thought we were crazy to do it, but now we can't keep up with demand for the screw cap version of our wine.

Indeed, making a difference often necessitates risk-taking. And not all risks pan out successfully. Nonetheless, at PlumpJack, we recognize that mistakes can be portals to discovery. With this in mind, we encourage our staff to be daring and to look for innovative approaches to running our restaurants, inns, and the winery.

We sure took a chance back in 1992, when we opened the original PlumpJack wine shop in San Francisco. Armed more with passion than experience, we improvised a lot and learned from the realities that presented themselves. Using my living room as the shop's case storage room wasn't a very good idea, for example. Sometimes I'd have to lock up the shop and go back home just to pick up wine for deliveries. But as our knowledge grew, so did our capacity for planning and innovation. It was good training for the challenges I've encountered throughout my career, both in food and wine as well as in public office.

The recipes in this book were selected from our broad portfolio, developed over time by the PlumpJack chefs in each of our restaurants. We hope that by using this book, you will be able to re-create the PlumpJack experience—from breakfast through dinner—in your own home.

My original passion for wine remains undiminished. Each bottle is an adventure—a blend of art and science, mystery and romance—unique, and so personal. At PlumpJack, we take this spirit of adventure and extend it to all of our properties. Our goal transcends food and wine. In a broad sense, we seek to provide our customers with memorable experiences that reflect our values and vision. Through the pages of this book, we invite you to take part in the rich culinary and visual tapestry that is PlumpJack today.

Gavin Newsom
Founder, The PlumpJack Group

The PLUMPJACK Cookbook

THE PLUMPJACK STORY

Back in 1992, a young food-and-wine-savvy entrepreneur named Gavin Newsom opened a small San Francisco wineshop with a mission to provide quality wines at reasonable prices. In the years that have passed, PlumpJack has grown to become a group of seven restaurants, two hotels, two wineshops, a winery, and a lounge—all situated in three distinct California locations: San Francisco, Napa Valley, and the mountain retreat known as Squaw Valley, not far from Lake Tahoe. The name PlumpJack is a nod to Shakespeare's Jack Falstaff, a freewheeling character who appeared in a number of the Bard's plays. "PlumpJack" is the nickname that Queen Elizabeth affectionately bestowed on Falstaff, whose girth was the result of an honest love of all things edible.

Diners enjoying themselves
at PlumpJack Cafe

The story of PlumpJack is one of West Coast ingenuity coupled with dedication and hard work. It starts in San Francisco and finishes—for the moment—with the recipes that comprise much of this book. They have been selected from the menus of PlumpJack's restaurants and cafes and include such signature recipes as the Balboa Burger and the famous Boon Fly Donuts as well as many dishes that capture the essence of the PlumpJack philosophy. Consider this opening chapter an introduction to that essence.

SAN FRANCISCO: PLUMPJACK'S BEGINNINGS

The PlumpJack crest graces the corner of the original wineshop.

The year was 1991. Twenty-three-year-old Gavin Newsom sat at the front corner table in his favorite San Francisco bistro, Balboa Cafe. He was commiserating with an old family friend, Pat Kelley, who at the time was employed at another restaurant on the verge of closing. Gavin has always been a good listener, so he encouraged Pat to tell her tales of woe.

Like Pat, Gavin was frustrated with his work. He had taken a job after college in property management. But his true passion was wine and food. Having grown up at the gateway to California's wine country, Gavin had come to appreciate Northern California's dynamic approach to eating and drinking well. The two friends were discussing their hopes and dreams when suddenly, in one of those "Eureka!" moments, Gavin blurted out, "Why don't we get a group of friends together and start a wineshop?"

It was an idea that clicked for both of them. Both Gavin and Pat wanted to break away from the somewhat rigid conventions they often encountered in the wine world. They were serious about fine wine, but they wanted to offer noteworthy wines at reasonable prices in an atmosphere that wasn't pretentious. Gavin set out to raise the money from a small group of like-minded friends and investors, while Pat looked for a suitable location for their new wine enterprise. Eventually, she found a commercial space across the street from Balboa Cafe, located in the neighborhood known as Cow Hollow.

It took them a year to put together the resources required for a start-up operation. With so much of their energy focused on the challenges of construction, government permits, and acquiring inventory, Gavin and Pat belatedly realized that they hadn't decided upon a name for their business.

One of their investors was longtime Newsom family friend Gordon Getty, the San Francisco philanthropist and composer. He had written an opera called *Plump Jack,* inspired by Shakespeare's Jack Falstaff. The budding wine merchants thought PlumpJack would make an appropriately fun and irreverent role model for the shop. They embraced the name along with the character's personality and incorporated a whimsical Elizabethan design—starting with the company crest—to give their new shop a unique look.

Whimsical décor provides a backdrop for a serious selection of fine wine at PlumpJack Wines.

PlumpJack Wines started with no employees. Gavin and Pat ran the shop themselves, as best they could. It was hard work, and as Gavin recalls, they were so understaffed that sometimes they would have to close the shop in order to make deliveries. Nonetheless, consumer response was very positive. Perhaps it was the casual, intimate, and friendly feeling shoppers encountered at the quaint store, coupled by an astute selection of cutting-edge wines, that made PlumpJack a "destination" rather than just another wineshop. Unimpressed by the so-called benchmark wines of the time, Gavin and Pat were drawn to lesser-known winemakers who would later become icons in their own right. As a result, there was a sense of discovery and innovation among the carefully stacked bottles and boxes. The same atmosphere, as well as Gavin's and Pat's philosophy of wine, sets the tone to this day. It's no wonder PlumpJack has become a magnet for consumers who come from near and far looking for a good bottle of wine at a price they can afford.

The pace of those early days proved both exhilarating as well as exhausting. After long hours on the floor selling or moving cases of wine, the two tired wine merchants would lock the door to their small shop and walk up the street to enjoy a snack at the nearby Balboa Cafe or—just a few doors away—at Pixley Cafe.

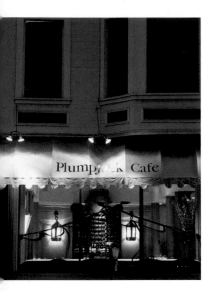

Fine wine led to fine dining at PlumpJack Cafe.

A Wineshop Leads to a Restaurant

Gavin believes you can't really enjoy wine without food. So it was only a question of time before he began thinking about starting a restaurant that featured the wines so thoughtfully acquired for the PlumpJack wineshop. In 1993, Pixley went up for sale, and Gavin determined to buy it. It was a financial stretch, but it fit into the wine merchant's philosophy of "undercapitalization," which Gavin says inevitably inspires a more creative form of entrepreneurship.

He needed to tap that creativity sooner than he ever imagined. The original restaurant plan was to create a PlumpJack wine bar that served "small plates" in a kind of Spanish tapas theme. But after completing the architectural and structural work required by the city's building safety codes, it became apparent that a casual wine bar would never pay back the investment. Something different needed to be done to bring in greater revenue without abandoning the PlumpJack credo of quality without pretense. What was required was a more upscale restaurant that still offered a comfortably casual dining experience.

Abandoning his wine bar concept, Gavin called the new restaurant PlumpJack Cafe. He figured that a cafe could be cozy and inviting while still serving a sophisticated cuisine in a somewhat formal setting. The look had to be sleek and contemporary. Yet it needed to appeal to both San Francisco's seasoned restaurant clientele as well as the new generation of up-and-coming twenty-somethings who were just beginning to reap the rewards of a dot-com economy. "Casual elegance" became the watchword, with classic white tablecloths highlighting white china and neatly placed silver. Fresh flowers at every table brought color to the dining tableau, as did the wines that flowed to every glass.

Echoing the wineshop's personality, the cafe atmosphere was intimate, with tables arranged to afford diners both space and privacy. Cream-colored walls provided a relaxing backdrop, lit with uniquely designed lighting fixtures inspired by the PlumpJack crest. Even the backs of the chairs were modeled after the whimsical shieldlike crest, contributing a consistency of style that prevailed throughout the room.

That consistency of style also emerged from the kitchen, which—from the very beginning—offered wine-friendly dishes inspired by California's seasonal bounty, a fast-growing coterie of local meat and produce purveyors, and a sense that pure, fresh ingredients were best highlighted by simple elegance. A salad of baby greens was tossed with local goat cheese and dressed in a vinaigrette made with Meyer lemons picked from a neighbor's garden and oil pressed from Napa Valley olives. Freshly caught Dungeness crab shared the menu with oysters farmed only twenty-five miles up the Pacific coast. Meats raised organically in nearby Marin and Sonoma Counties became kitchen staples, transformed by an innovative culinary team to exemplify the best of what is now loosely termed California cuisine. Early reviews were outstanding, and the restaurant quickly became one of San Francisco's hot new dining spots.

Gavin wanted to find a way to keep the price of his guests' meals in check. There was little he could do about the cost of high-quality ingredients and labor at the restaurant. To pay his bills, he would need to make certain margins on food. So he looked elsewhere for a line-item saving to pass along to diners. He found it in his wine list.

Typically, restaurant wine markups are a restaurateur's silver lining. Many restaurants charge their customers as much as double the retail price for a wine bottle. That's roughly three times what the restaurant pays to purchase the wine. It's a practice that limits many diners' enjoyment to lesser wines. Gavin felt that everyone eating in his restaurant should be able to enjoy a *good* bottle of wine with the food. To this end, the new PlumpJack Cafe offered wines at prices that were modeled on the retail prices at PlumpJack Wines—or nearly one-third less than a typical restaurant markup.

At the time, the move was revolutionary. PlumpJack Cafe's wine list prices found favor among local customers and also attracted the attention of local and national media. But not everyone was happy. Many other restaurateurs resented the move, fearing a backlash among customers at their own establishments. Some famous wineries were miffed as well. They thought their wines might appear to be undervalued, and several well-known vintners refused to sell more wine to PlumpJack. Despite the pressure, Gavin adhered to his ideals, and his wine-pricing philosophy found more favor than criticism in subsequent years.

Indeed, the formerly disgruntled winemakers have now renewed their relationship with PlumpJack, which again sells their wines at the wineshop and in the restaurant.

Ultimately, PlumpJack Cafe's initiative set off a far-reaching debate among restaurateurs and restaurant diners that has changed the way many restaurants sell wine today, and many restaurateurs now acknowledge the wisdom of selling more and better wine at lower prices.

BALBOA CAFE: A NEW RESTAURANT CHALLENGE

By 1995, PlumpJack Wines and PlumpJack Cafe were firmly established in the public eye as San Francisco food and wine meccas. Politicians, actors, artists, and other successful professionals were regularly seen *à table,* chowing down on the latest gourmet fare. The same chic city crowd would stop by the wineshop to purchase the latest and greatest vintage selections for evenings spent at home.

However, Balboa Cafe, where Gavin and Pat had originally hatched their wineshop plans, had fallen on hard times. The landmark restaurant first opened in 1913 and in its heyday served as a second home to the society crowd. But the new crop of socialites stopped patronizing Balboa as they had in the old days. The old luster had worn thin, and owner Jack "Slick" Hobday needed to sell. Balboa required an infusion of new energy and capital.

Gavin heard about Hobday's financial straits and couldn't resist the temptation to take on a new restaurant—especially one on the very same street as PlumpJack Wines and PlumpJack Cafe. The goal was to re-create the heart and soul of Balboa—that is, to reestablish it as a bustling, vibrant rendezvous for casual neighborhood interaction.

To do so, the PlumpJack Group kept the restaurant's basic design but gave it a face-lift that cleaned up a half century's worth of wear and tear. The great wooden bar that stretches throughout half the restaurant was carefully restored to its former glory. Tabletops were covered in white linen, incorporating the clean PlumpJack feel, but the redwood paneling and 1930s-style décor remained otherwise virtually unchanged. Today, from the outside, the corner restaurant looks set in a former era. Its grand neon sign is flanked by large red spheres emblazed with the Coca-Cola moniker. The original, simply painted signage is still in place at the rooftop's edge and reads "Balboa Cafe, Off Sale Liquors." Visually, Balboa provides us with a wonderfully direct connection to San Francisco's past.

In keeping with tradition, a few of the restaurant's signature dishes and drinks—like the Balboa Burger and famous Bloody Mary—remain on the menu. But many other offerings reflect PlumpJack's philosophy of fresh, locally grown ingredients. In contrast to PlumpJack Cafe's more formal, upscale culinary atmosphere down the block, prices at Balboa are kept lower, and the style is directed toward what is currently known as "comfort

Vintage neon and elegant crown molding herald Balboa's rich history.

food." Organically raised roast chicken and "skins-on" mashed potatoes are deftly paired with classic Cobb and Caesar salads. Hearty soups and slow-braised meats are highlighted along with traditional crab cakes. And to make sure no one feels rushed to leave, the bar stays open to 2 a.m., daily.

Balboa remains a very comfortable place to hang out. The local society movers and shakers have returned. But so have younger neighborhood residents in their blue jeans and short skirts. Regulars include former San Francisco mayor Willie Brown, plus local film stars like Sean Penn and Sharon Stone. But no one—regardless of fame or fortune—gets a reservation at Balboa Cafe. It's first come, first served. And that even applies to PlumpJack partner Gordon Getty, when he shows up for a Balboa Burger with the restaurant's signature pickled onions on the side. Waiting for a table among this illustrious crowd is half the fun of being there, of course. Fortunately, the long bar offers ample space for diners to indulge in a cocktail or glass of wine prior to their meal. In keeping with its neighborhood feel, the restaurant is open every day of the year, including Thanksgiving and Christmas, when as many as twenty turkeys or geese may be served.

Today, Pat Kelley spends much of her working day at Balboa. She likens Balboa to a giant dinner party where she knows all the guests. Since those heady early days, the Plump-Jack Group has opened another wineshop in San Francisco's Noe Valley and another restaurant called—not surprisingly—Jack Falstaff, located in the city's South of Market (SoMa) district. While expanding their enterprise, Gavin and his partners developed strong bonds with their food and wine purveyors. The local farmers provided them with a new sense of connection to the land as well as a desire to work on it. Gavin's original passion for wine led him to envision a vineyard and winery in the PlumpJack mold. His transition from wine merchant to winegrower was a natural one.

PLUMPJACK WINERY IS BORN

Surrounded by bottles of fine wines in his wineshop and restaurants and living some fifty miles from Northern California wine country, Gavin spent as much time as he could visiting with local winemakers at their vineyards and wineries. The hard-scrabble, down-to-earth work of growing grapes and the sheer artistry that ultimately emerged from a bottle of fine wine represented an intriguing process to him. As Gavin's knowledge and understanding of the annual winemaking cycle grew, so did his desire to produce a wine of his own. This creative urge soon became a mission, and in 1995, he discovered an underutilized Napa Valley vineyard and winery that he and his partners could transform and upgrade in the quest to make wine under the PlumpJack label.

The barrel room at
PlumpJack Winery

The winery had been built in the early 1880s and was located in the Oakville district, an area notable for rust red soils particularly well suited to growing Cabernet Sauvignon. Known as Villa Mount Eden, the vineyards had been used as a backdrop for the 1940 movie *They Knew What They Wanted,* starring Carole Lombard and Charles Laughton. (The film ultimately inspired Frank Loesser's 1956 Broadway musical, *The Most Happy Fella.*) But, like Balboa Cafe, the winery had seen better days and was ripe for new energy and direction.

Gavin and Gordon Getty kept the winery's basic infrastructure intact. The original exposed-wood-beam barrel room still serves as an integral part of the workspace, with rows of French oak casks snugly stacked and filled with the latest vintage. A new tasting room was built to accommodate the many visitors that flock to Napa Valley year-round. It is open seven days a week and, like Balboa Cafe, takes no reservations.

A charming courtyard forms the centerpiece of this quaint collection of small, artfully decorated buildings. Together, they create a seemingly casual environment for the very serious activity of making wine. During the fall harvest, presses, tanks, and barrels are in full use within just a few paces of the surrounding guest areas and vineyards. This close proximity to the winemaking team offers visitors an intimate view of the winemaking process.

The first PlumpJack wines were made in 1995. Since that time, the wines have received critical acclaim throughout the world. Regardless of praise, the goal has always been to make the best wines possible while honoring the integrity of the land. A full-time winery and vineyard crew employ sustainable growing methods to minimize the use of pesticides or other substances that might be harmful to the environment. In the winery, the best of Old and New World traditions help harvest the natural flavors of the grapes with as little human intervention as possible. The resulting varietals, which include Cabernet Sauvignon, Chardonnay, Merlot, Sauvignon Blanc, and Syrah, are a true expression of Napa Valley *terroir,* a word that evokes a sense of style that comes from the place where a wine is grown.

PlumpJack's new winery, Cade, set high on Howell Mountain, is scheduled to open later in 2007. The PlumpJack Group was named the management group of The Carneros Inn and two restaurants in the southern portion of the valley. In this ruggedly beautiful land of big sky and vine-studded hillsides, PlumpJack's winery, vineyards, hotel, and restaurants provide an ongoing seasonal connection to the Napa Valley wine country for all those who come to see, taste, and explore.

SQUAW VALLEY: A MOUNTAIN RETREAT

In 1985, Gordon Getty purchased a small ski lodge in Squaw Valley that had housed delegates to the 1960 Olympic Winter Games. Gordon renovated it, mostly for the convenience of housing friends and family in the mountainous area where he had enjoyed vacationing for many years.

Ten years later, as PlumpJack was expanding its reach from the original wineshop and restaurant to open other restaurants and the Napa Valley winery, the restaurants were receiving critical acclaim and business was good. To both Gordon and Gavin, Squaw Valley appeared to be an up-and-coming destination for lifestyle and dining pursuits that seamlessly fit the PlumpJack mold. And Gordon's Squaw Valley property seemed the ideal place to begin. The PlumpJack Group partners took over management and changed the name to the PlumpJack Squaw Valley Inn.

The inn underwent a sweeping physical transformation that incorporated the distinctive PlumpJack design. PlumpJack's shieldlike coat of arms and whimsical take on Elizabethan sensibilities set the tone. Artistically conceived lighting fixtures lent an

Blankets of snow frame the PlumpJack Squaw Valley Inn.

air of intimacy throughout the public areas, which also featured numerous nooks for congregating—from the grand circular fireplace beside the bar to the communal outdoor hot tubs that soothe muscles taxed by the rigors of skiing.

The inn is also home to PlumpJack Cafe Squaw Valley. Inspired by its San Francisco counterpart, PlumpJack Cafe Squaw Valley nonetheless offers its own distinctive dining experience. The look of both restaurants is similar, but the chefs arc free to create their own dishes. It's not unusual for them, as part of the PlumpJack culinary "family," to share recipes. But they also take the liberty of creating signature dishes based on locally available produce and other provisions. Typically, Squaw Valley diners have spent the day involved with some kind of intense physical activity, which means they are hungry. As a result, restaurant portions are usually robust.

There is drama here, too, for it seems that the breathtaking beauty of this mountain retreat stirs emotions. Tales of personal triumph on the slopes become animated at dinner, and it's not unusual to find several tables engaged in story swapping by evening's end. There was also the time when a young dinner guest stood up and loudly demanded the entire dining room's attention. He then dropped to his knees and publicly proposed marriage to his lovely dining partner. The scene ended happily with her resounding answer of yes.

PlumpJack has also opened a second Balboa Cafe in the village at Squaw Valley, nestled at the bottom of the steep ski slopes and only a minute's walk from the inn. Flush with sunshine at its high-altitude perch, this contemporary outpost of good living features boldly cut furnishings, hewn from massive timber. PlumpJack's sense of visual whimsy and its subtle nod to Elizabethan sensibilities remain, nonetheless, equally well integrated into this alpine expression of the PlumpJack mystique.

Balboa Cafe Squaw Valley offers the same casual climate as Balboa San Francisco—especially during the day, when ski or mountain bike attire is practically de rigueur. But for dinner, the white tablecloths are brought out to transform the restaurant into a slightly more formal affair replete with quiet conversation and the delicate clink of wineglasses. The bar, however, bustles with the gentle roar of late-night revelers, primed for a good time both on and off the slopes.

PlumpJack's move to Squaw Valley was prescient. Although the area had long offered challenging slopes to expert skiers, it was not yet the vacation hub it has become of late for families and individuals with a passion for living well when off—as well as on—the slopes. The formerly sleepy region now boasts a completely renovated alpine village built in the style of similar mountain communities throughout Europe. After more than a half century of fitful development, the area has created a sustainable niche for year-round enjoyment by both full-time residents as well as visitors—with a strong PlumpJack presence enhancing the local scene.

In the mountains, mealtime is the moment to gather and share tales of the day. With the PlumpJack and Balboa chefs in the kitchen, and with restaurant wine prices that don't defy gravity, the mood tableside is jovial. Surely Shakespeare's Jack Falstaff—aka Plump-Jack—would be at ease in the modern-day PlumpJack embrace, feasting into the wee hours of the night, and then retiring to his cozy bedroom. If it's true, as the great playwright said, that all the world's a stage, then Squaw Valley is PlumpJack's third act. From San Francisco to Napa Valley and the Sierra Nevada, PlumpJack strives to create memorable experiences anchored in the fine arts of food and wine.

Mealtime is the moment to gather and share tales of the day.

Skiers break for an al fresco libation in Squaw Valley's warm afternoon sunshine.

A PLUMPJACK WINE PRIMER

From its opening as a wineshop to its evolution as a winery and restaurant group, PlumpJack has always celebrated wine's impact on the way we eat. What wines should we enjoy most with our dinner? How do we define a wine's style? And why does wine taste the way it does?

These are all questions asked by anyone—from the novice to the expert—who wishes to better appreciate a glass of fine wine. And yes, there are other considerations. Even the shape of your glass can make a difference in your wine experience. Temperature plays a role, too. (Don't drink your red wines too warm; they're best between 60 and 70 degrees. And don't drink your white wines or rosés too cold; they show best between 50 and 55 degrees—or about ten minutes after removing them from the refrigerator.)

The Cabernet pick at harvest

The three questions in the first paragraph require some discussion. Use the tips, suggestions, and information that follow to further your enjoyment of this most intriguing of food-friendly beverages.

HOW WINE IS MADE

To begin, it helps to have a basic understanding of winemaking. Wine is, of course, fermented grape juice. The natural sugar in the juice is transformed by yeast to produce alcohol, which acts as a kind of flavor vector. That is, alcohol efficiently carries the many fruit flavors derived from the grapes across your palate. Exceptionally fruity wines are often referred to as "fruit-driven," even when they are dry. (This means that all the grape sugar has been converted to alcohol.) The alcohol also adds weight to a wine, giving it what is called "body." Typically, full-bodied wines are higher in alcohol than lighter-bodied wines.

Grape juice is essentially clear. Red wine gets its color from red grape skins, which macerate in the grape juice during fermentation. White wines are usually made from white grapes, which are generally pressed off the skins prior to fermentation. In other words, there is little or no "skin contact" in the white-wine fermentation process.

Sweet wines—which also have their place at the dinner table, most often as an aperitif or dessert—are made from very ripe grapes harvested late in the growing season, when they have the highest sugar content. Fermentation stops before the yeast has finished its work, leaving residual sugar in the wine. These late-harvest wines can be found in numerous styles, from lovely white late-harvest Rieslings and Sauvignon Blancs to dark red wines fortified with spirits and made in a manner similar to the Port wines of Portugal.

WHAT WINE SHOULD WE MOST ENJOY WITH OUR DINNER?

When considering that "perfect match" in food and wine pairing, you might want to entertain the possibility that none exists. Personal wine preferences and the inherent distinctions among wine varietals provide different but equally enjoyable ways to highlight the same dish. That's why one person may prefer Pinot Noir with grilled salmon, while another may favor Chardonnay. Both wines can serve up successful matches.

In pairing food and wine, what counts far more than a wine's color, grape variety, or even taste is its style or personality. Is the wine light or heavy? Bright or lush? Full-bodied or lean and crisp? These are words that define style. *As a general rule, a particular style of wine pairs well with a similar style of food.* That is, light-bodied, fresh, lively wines tend to go best

A Case for Decanting

While the clear glass bottles called decanters are hardly a requirement for the enjoyment of fine wine, diners at any of the PlumpJack restaurants can request a decanter to be brought tableside. The act of decanting a wine from its original bottle to a decanter may heighten drinking pleasure for several reasons.

Young wines—particularly red ones—can benefit from aeration. That's what happens when a wine is poured from a wine bottle into a decanter. Contact with air may soften coarse young tannins and also encourage the wine to "open up," or better reveal its flavors. Older wines, particularly reds, may contain bitter or unsightly solids that have dropped out of solution and are visible in the bottom of a bottle. For these wines, decanting offers a way to clarify the liquid prior to drinking.

How It's Done

Traditionally, an older wine is decanted by shining a candle or soft light under the bottle to illuminate its interior. However, it's fairly easy to see well enough inside a standard green wine bottle without the light. Slowly and steadily pour the contents of the original bottle into a decanter. Look for sediment as it collects in the shoulder of the original bottle and stop pouring just before the solids begin to escape. You may lose an ounce or two of wine in this manner, but your overall drinking experience will be vastly improved.

Decanting a young wine requires no special technique. Simply pour the liquid from one bottle to another. Unlike wineglasses, where shape is critical (see page 25), decanters require no specific form other than one that pleases you. Any glass bottle—even an old milk bottle—will do the job.

with lighter fare. Richer, full-bodied wines will best accompany richer or heavier meals. This complementary pairing guideline forms the foundation of matching wine with food.

Essentially, the natural acidity of all wines serves to balance the natural fats and oils present in nearly everything we eat. This natural acidity refreshes the palate and leaves it ready for another bite of food.

Typically, white wines have higher acidity than red wines, which makes them lighter and fresher in style. Chilling these wines softens their bright edge. Red wines, made from later-ripening red grapes that are higher in sugar than most white grapes, can be more full-bodied. They are generally lower in acidity and contain a bit more alcohol than white wines, which gives them more weight and roundness on the palate. As a rule, red wines are richer; white wines are brighter. Dry rosé—or pink wine—is usually made with red grapes but in a style more reminiscent of white wine. It falls somewhere between red and white and, not surprisingly, pairs well with a wide variety of foods. Sweet wines, with their concentration of sugar, are lush, viscous, and bold but may easily overwhelm the subtleties of many savory dishes.

Exceptions abound. Some red wines, such as Pinot Noir, come from grapes that ripen relatively early and are blessed with bright acidity. As a result, Pinot Noir makes a fine red-wine choice to accompany many lighter dishes like seafood and even certain salads. From an opposite tack, some white wines can serve up a lush fullness that matches the character of a red wine. For example, full-bodied, rich, buttery Napa Valley Chardonnay makes a good case for white wine with red meat.

Sometimes contrasting—not complementary—qualities provide a foil for a fine food and wine match. Take the richness of a plump oyster on the half shell. A bright-edged sparkling wine or a crisp, still white wine can provide the welcome contrast that a drop of lemon juice might otherwise offer. But the richness of a full-bodied Cabernet Sauvignon will probably ride roughshod over that poor oyster, creating a pairing most likely to disappoint.

In Cabernet Sauvignon and other red wines, tasters may discern an astringent or drying presence on the palate. This comes from tannins, chemical compounds present in grape skins and seeds. Because red wines are made with extended skin contact, they contain tannins. The tannins soften with time in the barrel and bottle, but they also will smooth out as they bond with proteins such as those found in a steak or a stew. When rough tannins meet juicy, rich red meats, the contrasting characteristics play off each other.

What about desserts or savory dishes that feature sweet ingredients such as fruit? Remember that dry wines are challenged by sweetness. So look for appropriate wines made in a sweet, or at least "fruit-forward," style to match the dish. An "off-dry"—or slightly sweet—Gewürztraminer may work well with mildly sweet Prosciutto with Port-Marinated Figs (page 61). Sweeter late-harvest Rieslings can marry beautifully with desserts such as Maple Crème Brûlée (page 182). And some full-bodied late-harvest Zinfandels or other red wines made in a Port style will match nicely with richer, more powerful chocolate treats.

By and large, if you can describe what you're eating in straightforward stylistic terms, you're likely to make a good choice when seeking an accompanying wine. Those dishes that are neither rich nor light, but somewhere in between—such as Seared Wild Salmon (page 118) or Pork Chops with Sweet Corn Maque Choux (page 141)—will be the most versatile as far as pairings go. These are dishes that work with a broad spectrum of wines ranging from whites to rosés and reds, too. The same holds true for "in-between" medium-bodied wines with modest acidity—regardless of color. Enjoy them with many of the dishes featured in this book.

Corks versus Screw Caps

The PlumpJack Experiment

Generating controversy and breaking new ground are long-standing San Francisco traditions.

As Napa Valley vintners, Gavin Newsom and Gordon Getty took a controversial position. In 2000, they put a screw cap—a closure generally associated with cheap jug wines—on their most expensive Napa Valley Cabernet Sauvignon. It was a move that rocked the wine establishment and set a precedent that is slowly but surely contributing to a change in the way wine is bottled.

In part, the screw cap was their response to the pretense and snobbery they sometimes encountered among wine aficionados. But even more important, the move was inspired by frustration arising from "cork taint," a pesky wine affliction that can make a perfectly good wine taste somewhat musty, bitter, or reduced in fruit flavor and aroma. Cork taint stems from a substance known as 2,4,6-trichloro-anisole (TCA), which can arise from the action of molds or other microorganisms on certain cork components. It is estimated that as much as 5 to 10 percent of all wine sealed with cork suffers from this defect. Would screw caps be an appropriate replacement for traditional cork?

The answer is still not clear, and the great cork debate continues to simmer. Discussion has grown less strident lately as more wines—many of them appreciated by knowledgeable collectors—have been released with screw cap closures. However, most wineries continue to bottle their reserve wines with a cork stopper while relegating screw caps to their second-tier labels.

Not so with PlumpJack. The winery bottles half of its highest-quality Reserve Cabernet Sauvignon with a screw cap and the other half with cork. The wine is sold in two-bottle packs that feature one of each type of closure. It is hoped that consumers will drink both wines together for comparison.

Currently, there appears to be little or no difference in the two wines. But it is premature to suggest that they will age long-term in exactly the same manner. A long-term aging study is presently underway at the University of California, Davis, to determine what the advantages or disadvantages may be to cellaring wine with either type of closure.

PlumpJack has no plans to abandon cork completely any time soon. The idea was to rock tradition, not abandon it. After all, what if it is ultimately determined that cork closures really are the best way to seal a wine for long-term cellaring?

Short-term, the most obvious advantage to using screw caps is that it dramatically reduces the risk of cork taint. It also simplifies the process of opening a bottle, although many wine lovers enjoy the time-honored ceremony of pulling the cork.

It's important to remember that many wines are best drunk young. That includes most white wines and rosés. Among these categories, look for an ever-increasing number of screw caps in the future.

HOW DO WE DEFINE A WINE'S STYLE?

As we learned on the previous pages, a wine's style may be defined in broad strokes. It can be full-bodied, weighty on the palate, lush, round, rich, and packed with ripe, black fruit flavors. Or it might be light-bodied, fresh, and bursting with tangy, bright acidity and citrus-like notes. Perhaps its style lies somewhere in between, which could make it a medium-bodied wine with moderate astringency and modest flavors. The key concepts here are body, texture, and intensity of flavor.

Acidity perks up your palate with tangy texture. Astringent, coarse tannins may dry out your mouth and give certain red wines a rough, rustic touch. Other red wines are blessed with firm, ripe tannins that produce a velvety sensation in your mouth. Some wines are sweet; some are dry. Some are fruity; we call them fruit-forward. Yet other wines are restrained—harder to taste—and grudgingly serve up very subtle flavor notes. We might refer to them as backward, or tight. If you can describe a wine's personality in general terms such as these, you have defined its style.

WHY DOES WINE TASTE THE WAY IT DOES?

Wine's complex layers of texture and flavor have intrigued generations of diners for thousands of years. Wine can be made from any fruit, but history has shown us that grapes provide the most interesting and exciting results.

Indeed, most wines are endowed with enough aromatic and taste components to stimulate the palate of anyone who likes to eat. These components are made up chiefly of chemical compounds known as esters and terpenes, also called essential oils. They are present, in varying degrees, among all members of the flowering plant world and give fruits their defining flavor characteristics.

Wine grapes contain a significant number of these natural flavoring agents, which enjoy increased potency postfermentation. When describing a favorite wine, critics typically unleash an avalanche of descriptors ranging from rose petals and currants to lemons, limes, and rosemary to chocolate and even coffee. Is it possible? Or have these tasters simply been caught up in a delirium for gustatory exaggeration? Actually, if you smell lavender, jasmine, and orange blossoms in your wine, you're probably not imagining it. Your nose has actually discerned specific chemical compounds redolent of those flowers and herbs.

Some 200-plus aromas and flavors have been identified in wine, but no one should try finding all of them. The best wines are identified by a more reasonable number of thematic smells and tastes. Young wines are often the fruitiest, with flavors that might remind us of

Fall colors in the vine in Napa Valley

grapefruit, lemon, lime, cherry, or raspberry. As wine ages, these primary flavors dissipate to reveal other secondary flavors—such as hazelnut, leather, and tea. Some wines are prized for their aging prowess, while others are best drunk when fresh and young. Personal taste also plays a role here, for not everyone appreciates the same qualities in a wine.

Oak barrels also contribute to the taste of wine. Barrel staves are toasted over an open flame, and that toasty quality can be imparted to wines aged in those barrels. There are also natural sugars in oak that caramelize during the toasting, which our noses may perceive as a hint of the burnt sugar flavor of crème brûlée. Ultimately, winemakers use oak the way chefs use salt and pepper to season a dish. Too much oak can be overpowering, but the right amount can highlight choice elements in a wine.

WINE VARIETALS

In California and much of the New World, wines are generally labeled with the name of the predominant grape that goes into the bottle. Chardonnay, Cabernet Sauvignon, and Pinot Noir, for example, are the names of grapes originally grown in Europe and now adopted by most of the world's wine-growing regions. Native American grapes such as Concords are a different species not particularly appreciated for outstanding wine quality.

In contrast to the American practice, Europeans traditionally label their wines by the region in which they are produced. In the Old World, grape varieties are blended according to longstanding regional traditions, and the blend is not often listed on the label.

As a Napa Valley winery, PlumpJack subscribes to the New World tradition of varietal designation. Sometimes different grapes are blended to create a wine that may be more interesting than one made from a single wine varietal. But by law, a wine labeled "Chardonnay" or "Cabernet Sauvignon" must contain at least 75 percent of the grape that appears on the label. Despite the fact that we rarely see much more than a dozen or so varietals on wineshop shelves, it's interesting to note that more than 100 different varieties of grapes are grown throughout California's vineyards. Many of those considered less distinctive are blended away without much fanfare.

Cabernet Sauvignon is the most widely planted red grape in Napa Valley. But many other fine locally grown varietals are produced as well, including Pinot Noir, Syrah, Sangiovese, Zinfandel, and Merlot. Among whites, Chardonnay is most popular, but Sauvignon Blanc, Pinot Blanc, and Viognier—among others—are also found in neighboring vineyards.

Each varietal has its own distinctive personality. However, there will be differences within a varietal depending on the climate where the grape is grown and the winemaking methods used. So a Cabernet from the Napa Valley, say, will probably have a different personality from one produced in New York, for example. The variability apparent in wines labeled with the same varietal designation is a welcome phenomenon. In fact, no two wines taste exactly the same. From bottle to bottle and year to year, every winery offers wine aficionados a fresh opportunity for discovery.

WHAT'S IN A GLASS?

Glassware affects the taste of wine. Here's why. About 90 percent of what we taste is really what we smell. So the way in which a wine's aromas reach our nose is critical to our appreciation of the beverage. Essentially, the aromas in wine are volatized, or carried up toward our nose through the air. A glass with edges that curve inward (concave) helps harness these aromas and direct them in a more precise manner toward our nostrils as they sniff for flavor.

And what about the many different shapes of wineglasses available today? From a consumer perspective, too many choices can be overwhelming. The best solution to the question of designer glassware is to find a shape—or several shapes—that appeal to you. After all, there's no sense in complicating what should essentially be a simple act of drinking pleasure.

Because a 5-ounce pour is common as a single serving, and because you don't want to fill your glass more than halfway (for reasons discussed below), 10 to 12 ounces is a good all-purpose size for home wine glassware. Larger wineglasses, which leave more head space to collect aromas, may enhance your drinking enjoyment, but they are hardly required for enjoying a good wine. Nonetheless, the larger glasses do add a certain special ambience to a meal graced with an excellent vintage.

The exception to standard wineglass guidelines are the tall, narrow glasses—often called flutes—that are used for sparkling wine. Bubbly is blessed with carbon dioxide, which efficiently carries aromas directly to your nose with little or no swirling required. The narrow glass provides a direct pathway to the bubbles. Feel free to fill your bubbly flute to the top.

A word about swirling wine in the glass prior to smelling and sipping: This is not some useless, esoteric custom but simply a way of aerating the wine, which facilitates the movement of aromas to your nose. In addition, swirling coats the sides of a glass with more wine, increasing the surface area of liquid in close proximity to your olfactory receptor. However, all of this swirling can be a messy affair if your glass contains too much wine. That's one reason seasoned wine drinkers rarely fill their glasses more than halfway. Another advantage to having adequate head space in your glass is that it serves as a kind of storage area for aromas that would otherwise quickly dissipate in the open air.

Harvest hues in the
PlumpJack vineyards

Breakfast

The great outdoors inspires healthy appetites. And for those who are exploring the Napa Valley vineyards or mountain pleasures of Squaw Valley, breakfast anticipates a full day's activities that might include anything from winery hopping to skiing or cycling.

At PlumpJack's Carneros and Squaw Valley inns, guests awaken to fresh-baked breads and pastries along with a full breakfast menu that will satisfy both light and serious eaters. In San Francisco, where late-night activities may require a lengthier morning sojourn in bed, Balboa Cafe offers brunch as a weekend option.

Breakfast is best when someone else makes it for you. But most of these recipes are reasonably simple and shouldn't greatly tax your early-morning disposition. A few items, like Lamb Hash Patties (page 45) and Roasted Banana Muffins (page 35), are more conveniently made in advance and reheated. PlumpJack Granola (page 30) requires some forethought as well. But it will last for weeks and serves as a quick, crunchy early-morning pick-me-up.

Regardless of where you may awaken, the recipes featured here are designed to whet your palate for a full day of serious fun.

PLUMPJACK GRANOLA

This crunchy, fruity, cinnamon-scented wake-me-up also makes a great midday snack—with milk and fresh fruit, or simply on its own. In Squaw Valley, it serves well as a trail mix during an alpine hike. Or try it as a topping for yogurt or ice cream.

PlumpJack Granola can be stored for up to three weeks in an airtight container, but it's usually consumed much faster. The greatest challenge is not eating all of it directly as it comes out of the oven! MAKES ABOUT 2½ QUARTS

¾ cup (1½ sticks) unsalted butter	¼ cup sesame seeds
1 cup honey	¼ cup flax or millet seeds
1 cup maple syrup	¼ cup unsweetened wheat germ
½ cup light corn syrup	¾ teaspoon ground cinnamon
4 cups rolled oats	½ teaspoon coarse salt
½ cup shredded coconut	1½ cups mixed dried fruit (any blend of raisins, cherries, cranberries, coarsely chopped apricots, figs, etc.)
½ cup chopped pecans	
½ cup slivered almonds	

Preheat oven to 350°F.

In a saucepan, combine the butter, honey, maple syrup, and corn syrup and slowly bring to a boil over medium heat. Reduce the heat and simmer for 5 minutes, stirring frequently. (Watch carefully; the liquid tends to boil over.)

In a large bowl, combine the oats, coconut, pecans, almonds, sesame and flax seeds, wheat germ, cinnamon, and salt. Pour the hot syrup mixture over the dry ingredients and combine thoroughly.

Lightly oil the surface of a large baking pan with canola oil, wiping off any excess with a paper towel. Spread the granola mixture evenly into the baking pan and bake for 15 minutes, stirring occasionally to prevent sticking or large clumps from forming. Remove the baking pan with the cooking granola from the oven and stir in the dried fruit, mixing it evenly. Return the baking pan to the oven and bake until golden brown, about 30 more minutes.

Let cool before sealing in an airtight container.

BOON FLY DONUTS The French would call these fluffy, round fried pastries *beignets*. Americans would probably describe them as donut holes. However, after one bite, you know you're munching on a bona fide donut, with its slightly sweet, vaguely chewy yet light-textured interior, surrounded by a dangerously delicious and almost crunchy cinnamon-sugar-coated outer shell. These morning treats are so good that guests at The Carneros Inn continue to order them all day long via room service from the neighboring Boon Fly Café.

If you want to make round, ball-shaped donuts, you'll need to maintain enough oil in the pan—a depth of about 2 inches—to allow them to float freely. Any less, and your donuts will flatten slightly, which is neither bad nor good. It's simply a question of preference. MAKES ABOUT 50 DONUTS, 2 INCHES IN DIAMETER

1 cup sugar	1 teaspoon coarse salt
¼ cup honey	½ teaspoon freshly grated nutmeg
¼ cup cane sugar syrup or light corn syrup	2 cups buttermilk
3 large eggs	4 tablespoons (½ stick) unsalted butter, melted
1½ teaspoons vanilla extract	2 tablespoons ground cinnamon
4 cups all-purpose flour	3 cups canola or vegetable oil, plus more as needed
1½ teaspoons baking powder	

In a large mixing bowl, combine ½ cup of the sugar, the honey, syrup, and eggs. Beat with an electric mixer at low speed to blend thoroughly. Stir in the vanilla.

In a separate large bowl, whisk together the flour, baking powder, salt, and nutmeg. Add half the flour mixture to the egg batter and beat with the mixer, continuing at low speed until well combined. Add 1 cup of the buttermilk and beat well, then add the remaining flour mixture. Once it is incorporated, beat in the remaining 1 cup buttermilk until the batter is smooth. Stir in the melted butter.

For best results, let the batter sit at room temperature for ½ hour to thicken before frying.

In a medium bowl, combine the cinnamon with the remaining ½ cup sugar. Have a plate lined with paper towels ready.

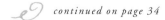 *continued on page 34*

Pour the canola oil to a depth of 2 inches into a large, heavy, deep sauté pan or skillet and heat over medium-high heat to 365°F, or until you can see small bubbles rising in the oil. Using a standard measuring spoon, spoon out tablespoon-size portions of the batter into the hot oil. Leave enough room for the donuts to float freely without bumping each other. (If necessary, reduce the heat to prevent the oil from splattering or smoking and add more oil if the level falls too much.) Depending on the size of your pan, you should be able to fry 10 to 15 donuts at a time.

Using a slotted spoon, flip the donuts when they turn golden brown at the edges, after 2 to 3 minutes. Fry until both sides are golden brown or deep tan, about 2 more minutes. Using the slotted spoon, transfer the donuts to the plate lined with paper towels. As soon as you can handle the donuts with your bare hands, roll them gently in the sugar and cinnamon mixture. Set them on a paper towel–lined serving plate or in a basket and serve at once, while they are warm.

ROASTED BANANA MUFFINS
On the heels of an evening's prandial extravagance, it's no wonder these subtly flavored, light-textured muffins are a breakfast hit with wine country guests at The Carneros Inn. Try them with a pat of butter and cappuccino on the side. Great for snacks, too. MAKES 12 MUFFINS

2 ripe bananas	½ teaspoon coarse salt
2 cups all-purpose flour	½ cup milk
1¼ cups sugar	1 large egg, beaten
2 teaspoons baking powder	4 tablespoons (½ stick) unsalted butter, melted
½ teaspoon baking soda	

Preheat oven to 400°F.

Make a 3-inch-long slice down each banana skin and lay the bananas on a baking sheet. Roast the bananas until the skins turn black and the juices in the bananas start to run from the slits in the skins, about 10 minutes. Remove the bananas from the oven but keep the oven on. When the bananas are cool enough to handle, discard the peels and place the bananas in a bowl or large, shallow dish. Mash with a fork and set aside.

In a large bowl, combine the flour, sugar, baking powder, baking soda, and salt and whisk to blend evenly. In another large bowl, whisk the milk, egg, and melted butter. Stir in the mashed banana. Thoroughly combine the dry ingredients with the banana mixture and stir with a wooden spoon to blend well.

Place a paper baking liner into each cup of a 12-tin muffin tray. Spoon the muffin batter into each cup, filling about three-quarters full. Bake until golden brown, or until a toothpick inserted comes out clean, 15 to 20 minutes.

The Boon Fly Café

A Casual Roadside Dining Spot

The red barnlike structure known as the Boon Fly Café beckons to hungry travelers on their way to and from the wine country. Named after an early local settler who shipped farm produce to San Francisco, the little cafe serves breakfast, lunch, and dinner from early morning to late evening. It's a casual, cozy place that caters to the many winemakers who work in the area as well as neighboring guests at The Carneros Inn who might be looking for a quick fix of locally inspired comfort food. The menu features a broad array of soups, salads, sandwiches, pastas, and main dishes, seasoned with herbs grown in gardens maintained by the inn. Unlike most roadside diners in America, this one features a wine list to make local vintners proud.

Boon Fly Café's signature donuts are legendary, whether enjoyed in the cafe or served piping hot to the inn's cottages via room service. But you don't have to come to Carneros to enjoy them. The recipe's right on page 32.

Smoked Salmon and Italian Fontina Frittata with Fresh Tarragon

Fresh tarragon fills the kitchen with its distinctive fragrance as it broils briefly atop this stylish egg dish, a close relative of an omelet, graced with salty, smoky-edged salmon and cheese.

Serve with buttered toast on the side or—with a little advance preparation—Oven-Roasted Potato "Fries" (page 91).

Frittatas start off on the stovetop like an omelet but finish under the broiler. Remember that the eggs will cook faster in a larger, shallower pan than in a smaller, high-sided pan. MAKES 4 SERVINGS

2 tablespoons extra virgin olive oil

1 cup diced red onion

8 large eggs

¼ pound smoked salmon, sliced into short, narrow strips

¼ pound Italian Fontina cheese, thinly sliced

¼ cup coarsely chopped fresh tarragon

Freshly ground pepper

Preheat broiler.

Heat the olive oil in a large flameproof skillet over medium heat until it shimmers. Cook the onion until it is translucent, about 3 minutes.

While the onion is cooking, crack the eggs into a large mixing bowl and whisk to blend thoroughly. Stir in the salmon.

Reduce the heat to medium-low, push the onion to the edge of the skillet, and pour in the egg/salmon mixture, making sure the salmon is evenly distributed throughout the egg. Use a wooden spoon or spatula to spread the onion back evenly throughout the egg. Lay the cheese slices in a circular pattern (like the hands of a clock) around the egg. Sprinkle the tarragon evenly over the top. Cook until the bottom of the egg has set, 3 to 5 minutes. The top of the egg should still be runny.

Remove the skillet from the stovetop and place it on the top oven rack directly under the broiler. Cook the frittata until it is sizzling and the surface has taken on a golden brown hue, 3 to 5 minutes.

Remove the skillet from the oven, cut the frittata into quarters, and serve immediately, garnished with freshly ground pepper to taste.

Poached Eggs with Canadian Bacon, Potato Pancakes, and Lemon/Herb Cream Sauce

A tangy lemon/ herb cream sauce and smoky Canadian bacon (which is really cured pork loin) set this apart from traditional ham 'n' eggs. You can substitute any favorite ham for Canadian bacon. The crispy potato pancakes are enhanced by the addition of leeks. Give yourself a little extra time in the kitchen, as there is some multitasking required. Think of it as part of your morning recreation. The result is worth the effort. MAKES 4 SERVINGS

AND IN YOUR GLASS

ANY LIGHT, VIVACIOUS, DRY WHITE WINE WILL DO NICELY HERE, AS IT STRIKES A FINE BALANCE WITH THE LEMON/HERB CREAM SAUCE. TRY SAUVIGNON BLANC OR PINOT GRIGIO—OR PLUMPJACK'S LEGENDARY BLOODY MARY (PAGE 47).

FOR THE POTATO PANCAKES

2 russet potatoes (about 12 ounces each)	1 small leek, white part only, thinly sliced (about ½ cup)
4 tablespoons extra virgin olive oil	2 tablespoons all-purpose flour
1 large egg	½ teaspoon coarse salt

Preheat oven to 350°F.

Set the potatoes directly on the oven rack and bake for 30 minutes. Pierce them with a fork to check for doneness. They should still be firm and almost—but not fully—cooked.

As soon as the potatoes are cool enough to handle, peel them, shred on the large holes of a box grater, and place them in a large bowl. Add 2 tablespoons of the olive oil, the egg, leek, flour, and salt. Use your hands to thoroughly mix all the ingredients and form into 8 patties.

In a large skillet or sauté pan, heat the remaining 2 tablespoons olive oil over medium-high heat until it shimmers. Place the patties in the pan and cook until golden brown, 5 to 7 minutes per side.

FOR THE CREAM SAUCE

1 tablespoon extra virgin olive oil	1 cup heavy cream
¼ cup diced shallots	4 tablespoons (½ stick) unsalted butter, cut in pieces
½ cup white wine	
¼ cup white wine vinegar or apple cider vinegar	1 tablespoon minced fresh chives
	1 tablespoon minced fresh tarragon
Zest of 1 lemon, removed with a vegetable peeler and minced	Coarse salt

Prepare the sauce while the potatoes are baking.

continued on page 42

In a small saucepan, heat the olive oil over medium heat until it simmers. Add the shallots and cook until they are translucent, about 3 minutes. Add the wine, vinegar, and lemon zest and bring to a boil. Reduce the heat to medium-low and cook until most of the liquid has evaporated and the pan appears almost dry. Stir in the cream, bring to a simmer, and continue to cook, stirring occasionally, until the liquid is reduced by half, about 15 minutes. Remove the pan from the heat. Stir in the butter until it melts. Stir in the chives and tarragon, season with salt to taste, cover, and reserve.

TO SERVE

> 1 tablespoon white wine vinegar or apple cider vinegar
>
> 8 large eggs
>
> 8 slices Canadian bacon, grilled or fried
>
> Freshly ground pepper

While the potato pancakes are cooking, fill a large, wide, deep sauté pan with 3 inches of water. Add the vinegar, bring to a boil, then reduce to a strong simmer. When the pancakes are almost ready to eat, gently crack the 8 eggs into the simmering water and cook for 3 minutes. Quickly reheat the cream sauce over medium-high heat if it has cooled.

Place 2 slices of the Canadian bacon on each of 4 plates. Use a slotted spoon to carefully remove each egg from the water and place 1 on top of each ham slice. Nap each egg with the cream sauce and place 2 potato pancakes on each plate so that they are just touching the sauce and eggs.

Serve immediately, with freshly ground pepper to taste.

BUTTERMILK PANCAKES There is a certain yin/yang pleasure derived from the pairing of tart and sweet. On its own, buttermilk tastes a bit like liquid yogurt, with its bright-edged kick and tart aftertaste. The cultured milk gives these fluffy, light pancakes a tangy quality that pairs beautifully with warm maple syrup. When wild blackberries are in season, the PlumpJack chefs love to lace this breakfast treat with the local bounty. Other fruits such as blueberries, raspberries, and sliced bananas make fine additions as well.

The batter appears thick and somewhat lumpy, which is normal. Add a touch more buttermilk or regular whole milk if it becomes too thick in the bowl as you cook batches of pancakes. MAKES ABOUT 32 PANCAKES, 3 INCHES IN DIAMETER

2 cups all-purpose flour	½ cup milk
1½ teaspoons sugar	2 tablespoons unsalted butter, melted, plus more for serving
2 teaspoons baking powder	
½ teaspoon baking soda	1 cup wild blackberries (optional)
¾ teaspoon coarse salt	Canola or vegetable oil
2 large eggs, beaten	Warm maple syrup, for serving
2 cups buttermilk	

In a large bowl, whisk together the flour, sugar, baking powder, baking soda, and salt.

In a separate large bowl, whisk together the eggs, buttermilk, milk, and melted butter. Use a wooden spoon to stir the buttermilk mixture into the flour mixture, blending until the dry ingredients are moistened (some lumps are fine). Stir in the blackberries, if using.

Heat a griddle or a heavy skillet over medium-high heat. Brush the griddle with canola oil (or use paper towels), coating it evenly.

Ladle enough batter onto the griddle to create pancakes that are about 3 inches in diameter. Cook them until they bubble on the top and are golden brown on the bottom. Flip them and cook for another minute or two, until both sides are golden brown. Repeat with the remaining batter, oiling the griddle as needed. (Monitor pan temperature closely to keep it as hot as possible without smoking.)

Serve each batch immediately, or keep the pancakes warm in a preheated 250°F oven until all the batter has been cooked. This way, everyone can eat together. Serve with butter and warm maple syrup.

Huevos Rancheros with Tomato and Fresh Cilantro Salsa

This classic Mexican version of fried eggs makes a perfect breakfast, but it can also double as lunch or dinner. Extra virgin olive oil adds a subtle fruity note to the ensemble, which is topped with a zippy bright tomato and cilantro salsa.

To make your morning easier, try preparing the salsa the night before. For best results, all the ingredients (except the cheese and the avocado) should be piping hot. It's easiest to make huevos rancheros in small batches for one or two diners at a time. The recipe below serves two. Double it for a foursome. MAKES 2 SERVINGS

FOR THE SALSA

2 cups coarsely chopped ripe tomatoes

1 cup diced onion

1 cup packed coarsely chopped fresh cilantro

½ jalapeño pepper, seeded and coarsely chopped

Juice of ½ lemon

½ teaspoon coarse salt

Place the tomatoes, onion, cilantro, jalapeño, lemon juice, and salt in a food processor and pulse to make a coarse puree. Cover and refrigerate for up to 3 days. (Makes about 2 cups.)

AND IN YOUR GLASS

FOR AN EXCELLENT BRUNCH, ENJOY THIS DISH WITH PLUMPJACK'S LEGENDARY BLOODY MARY (PAGE 47).

FOR THE EGGS

2 cups cooked black beans (page 200) or 1 can (15 ounces) black beans

3 tablespoons extra virgin olive oil

4 large eggs

2 flour tortillas (8 inches in diameter)

½ cup shredded Monterey Jack or white Cheddar cheese

½ ripe avocado, pitted but not peeled

Coarse salt

In a small pot, heat the beans over medium-high heat, stirring occasionally. When hot, cover and reduce the heat to low, stirring now and then to prevent the beans from sticking to the pot.

In a medium skillet, heat 1 tablespoon oil over medium-low heat. Crack the eggs into the pan and cook until the whites are fairly solid but the yolks are still yellow and runny, 3 to 5 minutes.

While the eggs are cooking, heat the remaining 2 tablespoons oil in another skillet over medium-high heat. Lay 1 tortilla in the hot oil and fry on each side until slightly brown and slightly puffy, about 30 seconds per side. (If the oil starts to smoke, reduce the heat.) Place on a paper towel to drain. Repeat for the second tortilla.

Lay each hot tortilla on a plate. Spread approximately ⅔ cup beans over each. Sprinkle grated cheese to taste (3 to 4 tablespoons per serving) over the beans and place 2 eggs on top of the cheese. Garnish the eggs with 2 to 3 tablespoons salsa, depending on your taste. Scoop a few tablespoons of avocado onto the side of each plate and sprinkle with salt to taste. Serve immediately.

Lamb Hash Patties with Poached Eggs

This hearty wake-up dish will prepare you for a full morning's activities. Bite-size chunks of rich, earthy lamb are framed neatly in a patty-shaped bed of potatoes that's crunchy on the outside and soft inside. The poached egg serves simultaneously as a garnish and a colorful sauce, as the soft, silky yolk drizzles down the side of the patties.

Unless you are getting up very early, make the patties a day in advance. Store them overnight in the refrigerator and then simply sauté for 10 minutes, while your coffee is brewing. MAKES 6 SERVINGS

AND IN YOUR GLASS

NOT SURPRISINGLY, LAMB AND EGGS CAN STEP OUT OF THE BREAKFAST ARENA AND STAND IN QUITE NICELY FOR LUNCH OR DINNER. ON THESE OCCASIONS, TRADE IN YOUR COFFEE CUP FOR A GLASS OF EQUALLY HEARTY RED WINE SUCH AS CABERNET SAUVIGNON OR ZINFANDEL. LIGHTER (AND TYPICALLY LOWER IN ALCOHOL) REDS LIKE PINOT NOIR AND SANGIOVESE MIGHT WORK BEST AT LUNCHTIME, ESPECIALLY IF YOU'VE GOT A BUSY AFTERNOON SCHEDULED.

FOR THE LAMB HASH

4 tablespoons extra virgin olive oil

1 pound lamb shoulder, cut into cubes

¼ cup white wine, plus more if necessary

¼ cup diced onion

¼ cup diced carrot

¼ cup diced celery

1½ cups chicken stock (page 194) or canned low-sodium chicken broth

Coarse salt

1 bay leaf

½ teaspoon black peppercorns

2 medium russet potatoes (about ½ pound)

½ cup diced red bell pepper

1 tablespoon minced jalapeño pepper

1 teaspoon dried thyme

1 teaspoon dried tarragon

Freshly ground pepper

Preheat oven to 350°F.

In a Dutch oven or other large ovenproof pot, heat 1 tablespoon of the olive oil over medium-high heat until it shimmers. Brown the lamb cubes in the oil on all sides, about 2 minutes per side. Pour the white wine into the pot and stir to release any bits of meat that may be stuck to the bottom. Add the onion, carrot, and celery and cook, stirring occasionally, for 1 minute. Add the chicken stock, 1 teaspoon salt, the bay leaf, and peppercorns and bring to a boil. Cover the pot and bake until the meat is tender, about 1½ hours.

After 1 hour, place the potatoes in the oven and bake them for 30 minutes. Pierce them with a fork to check for doneness. They should still be firm and almost—but not fully—cooked. Remove the potatoes and the meat (which should be done) from the oven at the same time. Let the meat and potatoes cool until you can handle them with your bare hands. Discard the other solids from the pot.

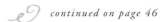 *continued on page 46*

Using your hands, pull the meat into shreds and reserve. Peel the potatoes, shred them on the large holes of a box grater, and reserve in a large bowl.

Heat 1 tablespoon of the oil in a large skillet over medium heat. Cook the bell pepper and jalapeño until the bell pepper is somewhat tender, about 1 minute. Stir in the thyme and tarragon. Add the lamb and stir to mix well with the peppers. Cook for 2 to 3 minutes, to combine the flavors. If the lamb starts to stick to the pan, add an additional ¼ cup white wine to release any bits stuck to the bottom. Season with salt and pepper to taste, set aside, and let cool for 5 to 10 minutes.

Add the lamb to the potatoes and use your hands to combine. Form the hash into 6 patties. (If you are planning to eat these patties later on or the following day, wrap each one in plastic wrap and refrigerate for up to 36 hours.)

In a large skillet or sauté pan, heat the remaining 2 tablespoons olive oil over medium-high heat until it shimmers. Place the patties in the pan and cook until golden brown, 5 to 7 minutes per side.

TO SERVE

1 tablespoon apple cider or white wine vinegar	6 large eggs

While the patties are cooking, fill a large, deep sauté pan with 3 inches of water. Add the vinegar and bring to a boil. Reduce to a strong simmer.

When the patties are almost done, gently crack the eggs into the simmering water. Cook the eggs for 3 minutes.

Place a patty on each of 6 plates. Using a slotted spoon, carefully remove the eggs from the water and place on top of a patty. Serve immediately, with freshly ground pepper to taste.

PlumpJack's Legendary Bloody Mary

Before PlumpJack even existed, Balboa Cafe's Bloody Mary was a legendary brunch tradition in San Francisco's Cow Hollow district. The old recipe was saved and is now used in many of the PlumpJack dining establishments, including Balboa Cafe, where it still highlights Sunday brunch.

Typically, vodka is the spirit of choice. But a Bloody Mary made with gin will be perfumed by gin's exotic collection of herb and spice qualities. Try a comparative tasting to determine your preference.

If possible, use a low-sodium organic tomato juice instead of the highly salted commercial brands more commonly found in the marketplace. Better juice will yield a purer expression of flavor in your glass. Pickapeppa—a distinctive Jamaican sauce—is available in many specialty stores. MAKES 4 DRINKS

1 quart tomato juice	½ teaspoon red Tabasco sauce
2 tablespoons fresh lemon juice	½ teaspoon green Tabasco sauce
1 teaspoon Pickapeppa sauce	4 ounces vodka or gin
1 teaspoon Worcestershire sauce	4 lemon wedges
1 teaspoon prepared horseradish	4 sticks celery (6 to 8 inches long)

Pour the tomato juice into a large pitcher. Stir in the lemon juice, Pickapeppa sauce, Worcestershire sauce, horseradish, and both Tabasco sauces.

Fill 4 tall glasses (12 to 14 ounces) about one-third full with ice cubes. Add the Bloody Mary mixture to each glass, leaving enough room for the vodka and garnishes.

Add 1 ounce vodka (or gin) to each glass and stir. Place a lemon wedge and a celery stick in each glass and serve.

STARTERS, SALADS, SOUPS, AND SIDES

Small plates can serve up a large measure of satisfaction, with appetizers and salads setting the stage for more good things to come. They warm up the palate and allow us to ease into a meal. It's not unusual for a first course to stand in stark contrast to a main course. As such, an appetizer presents us with the option of choosing an introductory wine as well—one that pairs most effectively with the first part of a multifaceted meal.

Of course, appetizers and salads can also stand in as the main course for a more modest meal. Cobb Salad (page 56) makes a fine lunch on its own. Mushroom Pizza with Caramelized Onions (page 68) would satisfy most of us as a centerpiece for lunch or dinner, especially when preceded by a simple salad of Baby Greens with Lemon Vinaigrette (page 50) or a Caesar Salad (page 51). Soups work beautifully as starters or as main attractions, too, often accompanied by country breads like Focaccia Bread with Fresh Rosemary (page 84), or possibly the Grilled Portobello Mushroom Sandwich (page 62). Perhaps most versatile of all are the side dishes featured at the end of this chapter. The PlumpJack chefs pair them admirably with many of the main courses highlighted throughout these pages.

Baby Greens with Lemon Vinaigrette

This light, lemony salad offers a refreshing alternative to traditional green salad. It uses no vinegar. Instead, lemon juice provides the acid backbone. Lemon zest gives extra lift, while crunchy shallots provide additional texture. It's simple yet elegant—an excellent introduction to any meal. MAKES 4 FIRST COURSE SERVINGS

2 tablespoons fresh lemon juice

Zest of 1 lemon, minced

3 tablespoons extra virgin olive oil

1 teaspoon Dijon mustard

1 small shallot, minced

Pinch of coarse salt

Freshly ground pepper

4 ounces baby lettuce greens or 1 medium head butter lettuce

In a small bowl, whisk together the lemon juice, lemon zest, olive oil, mustard, shallot, salt, and pepper.

Place the baby greens in a large salad bowl and drizzle with the dressing. Toss well to coat evenly. Serve immediately.

CAESAR SALAD

Caesar salad can be made in many styles. This light and lemony version is probably the most popular salad served at Balboa Cafe. It makes a fabulous opener to any meal, refreshing the palate with each bite. Croutons may be a classic component here, but don't overdo it. A little crunch adds interest; too much can be distracting. MAKES 4 TO 6 FIRST COURSE SERVINGS

FOR THE DRESSING

2 anchovy fillets

1 egg yolk (see note below)

1 cup extra virgin olive oil

½ clove garlic, minced

2 cloves roasted garlic (page 191)

Juice of 2 lemons (about ⅓ cup)

¼ cup freshly grated Parmesan cheese

¼ teaspoon coarse salt (optional)

Place the anchovies, egg yolk, olive oil, and the raw and roasted garlic in a blender or food processor and pulse to blend. Blend in the lemon juice.

Scrape the dressing into a bowl or jar and stir in the cheese. Add the salt, if desired.

FOR THE SALAD

2 Romaine lettuce hearts

1 to 2 cups homemade croutons
(page 198)

Freshly ground pepper

Place the lettuce and croutons in a large salad bowl. Add half the dressing and toss thoroughly. Add more dressing to taste. Garnish the salad with freshly ground pepper to taste.

Any leftover dressing can be refrigerated, covered, for up to 2 days.

Note: Typically, Caesar salad dressing is made with raw egg yolks, which have been linked on rare occasions to salmonella poisoning. As a result, small children, older individuals, or anyone with a compromised immune system should probably avoid them. Fortunately, fresh eggs from a reputable source pose little risk for most of us.

AND IN YOUR GLASS

DRESSED IN A BRIGHT, TANGY LEMON VINAIGRETTE, THIS SALAD CRIES OUT FOR A SIMILARLY ZIPPY WINE. CHILLED BUBBLY OR A FRESH-TASTING, MINERAL-LIKE CHARDONNAY WOULD SERVE NICELY HERE.

Avocado and Grapefruit Salad with Toasted Almonds and Sherry/Citrus Vinaigrette

This is a refreshing juxtaposition of textures and tastes. Crunchy almonds, tangy grapefruit, and a subtle hint of spice from the chile all play in contrast to the avocado's creamy richness. Salty, nutty Manchego (a sheep's-milk cheese from Spain) highlights the ensemble. MAKES 4 FIRST COURSE SERVINGS

FOR THE VINAIGRETTE

¼ cup amontillado sherry	2 shallots, sliced
½ cup water	Juice of 2 oranges
2 ancho chiles, stemmed, seeded, and crushed or coarsely chopped (see note below)	Juice of 1 lime
	½ cup extra virgin olive oil

AND IN YOUR GLASS

GIVEN THE SHERRY FOUNDATION OF THE VINAIGRETTE, THIS SALAD PAIRS BEAUTIFULLY WITH A GLASS OF CHILLED FRUITY BUT DRY SHERRY.

In a saucepan, bring the sherry and water to a boil. Add the chiles and shallots, lower the heat to simmer, and reduce the liquid by half. Strain into a bowl; discard the solids.

Pour the orange and lime juices into a separate bowl. Add the sherry reduction and stir in the olive oil. Set aside.

FOR THE SALAD

1 small head butter lettuce	½ cup slivered almonds, toasted (page 192)
2 ripe avocados, seeded, peeled, and cut into ⅛-inch slices	¼ pound Manchego cheese, cut into thin slivers
1 grapefruit, peeled, sections separated	Freshly ground pepper

Place a few lettuce leaves on each of 4 salad plates. On top of the leaves, arrange the avocado slices and grapefruit sections in a circle, alternating the avocado and grapefruit wedges to form a kind of pinwheel design. Top with a sprinkling of almonds and several slivers of cheese. Drizzle with the sherry/citrus vinaigrette. Season with freshly ground pepper to taste.

Note: The ancho is a dried, ripened poblano, dark red and wrinkled in appearance. It is also known as a pasilla in some parts of the country.

Beet Salad with Arugula, Feta Cheese, Toasted Pistachios, and Orange/Tangerine Vinaigrette

Earthy, sweet red and golden beets sit snugly with spicy greens topped with tangy feta cheese and crunchy, smoky pistachios to create a fine blend of color and texture. When it is available, the PlumpJack chefs often use mizuna, a Japanese green similar to peppery arugula but a bit more subtle. MAKES 4 FIRST COURSE SERVINGS

AND IN YOUR GLASS

SWEET BEETS, TANGY CITRUS, AND SPICY GREENS SERVE UP A COMPLEX BLEND OF EXCITING FLAVORS HERE. CHOOSE A WINE WITH FIRM ACIDITY AND POSSIBLY A HINT OF SWEETNESS TO BEST ENHANCE THIS DISH. A BARREL-FERMENTED CHARDONNAY OR CHENIN BLANC WOULD SERVE WELL. SO WOULD A RIESLING, A GEWÜRZTRAMINER, OR EVEN A LIGHTLY SPARKLING LATE-HARVEST MUSCAT.

FOR THE BEETS

3 red beets	3 golden beets

Preheat oven to 400°F. If beet greens are attached, remove them, leaving about ½ inch of the stalks. Do not peel the beets.

Wrap the red and golden beets separately in aluminum foil, leaving the top of the foil open. Roast them until they are tender when pierced by a fork, about 1 to 1½ hours, depending on the size of the beets. When the beets are cool enough to handle, peel the skins and remove the tops. Cut the peeled beets into quarters or eighths and set aside.

FOR THE VINAIGRETTE

Juice of 1 orange	1 teaspoon fennel seeds
Juice of 2 tangerines	1 sprig tarragon
1 shallot, thinly sliced	½ cup extra virgin olive oil

In a small saucepan over high heat, bring the orange juice, the juice of 1 tangerine, the shallot, fennel, and tarragon to a boil. Lower the heat to medium and reduce by half. Strain into a small mixing bowl and discard the solids. Whisk in the olive oil and the remaining tangerine juice.

FOR THE SALAD

4 to 6 ounces arugula or mizuna	¼ cup pistachios, toasted (page 192)
¼ cup feta cheese, crumbled	Coarse salt and freshly ground pepper

Lay a bed of arugula on 4 salad plates. Divide the red and golden beets evenly on top of the greens. Top the beets with the feta cheese and pistachios. Whisk the vinaigrette one last time and drizzle 1 to 2 tablespoons over each salad. Or you can top the beets with the greens and cheese, as in the photo. Season with salt and pepper to taste.

COBB SALAD Essentially a California take on Niçoise salad, Cobb salad was created at the original Brown Derby restaurant in Hollywood. According to legend, the salad was first made one late night back in 1937 when the owner, Bob Cobb, was rummaging about in his refrigerator looking for a snack. He found some lettuce, an avocado, hard-cooked eggs, tomatoes, a cold breast of chicken, bacon, a few other items, and some "French" dressing. He then shared his salad with Sid Grauman (of Grauman's Chinese Theatre), who asked for it again the following day, calling it Cobb Salad. As they say in Hollywood, a star was born.

We've improved on Cobb's original dressing. Ours is creamy rich, yet also tangy bright from the two different vinegars. A touch of honey balances the brightness and gives just a hint of sweetness. Mixed baby salad greens yield the best results, although any fresh greens will do. MAKES 4 MAIN COURSE SERVINGS

AND IN YOUR GLASS

WITH ITS CREAMY
DRESSING, HINTS OF
HONEY AND BACON, AND A
STELLAR CAST OF EGGS,
CHICKEN, AND FRESH
GREENS, THIS CORNUCOPIA
OF TASTES PAIRS WILDLY
WELL WITH A FRUITY WHITE
WINE SUCH AS RIESLING
OR GEWÜRZTRAMINER.
MORE MAINSTREAM
CHARDONNAY OR
SAUVIGNON BLANC WILL
DO NICELY HERE, TOO. DRY
ROSÉ ALSO STEPS UP
TO THE PLATE WITH
DISTINCTION.

FOR THE DRESSING

2 slices bacon, cut into ½-inch pieces

2 tablespoons sherry vinegar

2 tablespoons red wine vinegar

2 teaspoons whole-grain mustard

¼ cup crème fraîche

2 teaspoons chopped fresh thyme or 1 teaspoon dried thyme

1 tablespoon honey

¼ cup extra virgin olive oil

¼ cup canola oil

Place the bacon in a saucepan and cover with water. Bring to a boil and let the water evaporate to help render the fat. When the water has evaporated, continue cooking the bacon over medium heat until it begins to brown, 2 to 3 minutes. Remove the pan from the heat and carefully pour out any excess fat. Add the vinegars to the pan and stir to release any bits of bacon that might be stuck to the pan.

Scrape the bacon and vinegars into a blender or food processor. Add the mustard, crème fraîche, and thyme and blend until smooth. Add the honey, olive oil, and canola oil and pulse to emulsify. Cover and refrigerate until ready to use, or for up to 3 days. (Makes about 1 cup.)

FOR THE SALAD

1 whole boneless, skinless chicken breast

Course salt and freshly ground pepper

1 tablespoon extra virgin olive oil

4 slices bacon

8 to 10 ounces mixed baby salad greens

4 large eggs, hard-cooked

1 avocado, pitted, peeled, and sliced

1 cup cherry tomatoes, halved

½ cup blue cheese, crumbled

Season the chicken breast with salt and pepper. In a saucepan or small skillet, heat the olive oil over medium-high heat until it shimmers. Sauté the chicken breast until it is just cooked through, 7 to 10 minutes per side. Set aside.

In another pan, cook the bacon over medium-high heat, turning the slices occasionally, until they are crisp and brown. Set aside on paper towels to drain. Crumble into bacon bits when cool enough to handle.

In a large salad bowl, toss the baby lettuce greens in half of the dressing. Evenly divide the greens among 4 large, shallow bowls or plates.

Cut the eggs in quarters and arrange them in a pinwheel shape on top of the lettuce. Cut the chicken breast into thin slices and intersperse them with the egg. Do the same with the avocado slices. Garnish with the tomatoes, blue cheese, and bacon bits. Pass the remaining dressing at the table.

AHI CRUDO WITH THREE SALADS

As the Japanese have long known, eating raw fish can be quite sensual. The Italians also enjoy raw fish, and this recipe blends both traditions.

In this dish, three simple salads highlight the tuna. Each salad has a distinct character, which allows the diner to experience the same fish in three very different ways. Don't obscure these pretty salads by covering them with too much tuna. Two or three slices of fish, artfully arranged over each salad mound, will lead to a refreshingly pleasing visual as well as gustatory experience.

Ahi tuna has a mild, subtle flavor and a silky texture. Use only very fresh sashimi-grade tuna purchased from a reputable fishmonger. MAKES 4 FIRST COURSE SERVINGS

AND IN YOUR GLASS

IN KEEPING WITH THE SUBTLE DELICACY OF THE DISH, PAIR IT WITH AN EQUALLY DELICATE WHITE WINE SHOWING BRIGHT ACIDITY AND LITTLE, IF ANY, OAK. A CHILLED HIGH-END SAKE WOULD ALSO WORK WELL HERE.

FOR THE FENNEL AND ORANGE SALAD

1 fennel bulb, very thinly sliced

1 orange

1 teaspoon extra virgin olive oil

Set the fennel aside in a medium bowl. Use a vegetable peeler to remove the zest from the orange. Slice the zest into very narrow strips 1 to 2 inches long. Add the zest to the fennel and toss with the olive oil. Cut as much of the white pith off the orange as you can. This will help you see the membrane dividing the segments. Slice 6 to 8 segments free from between the connecting membrane. Reserve the segments. Squeeze the juice from any remaining uncut orange into the fennel and orange zest, and toss again. Cover and refrigerate until ready to use.

FOR THE RADISH AND OLIVE SALAD

1 bunch radishes (12 to 14 radishes)

⅓ cup pitted olives, such as kalamata, chopped

Leaves from 3 or 4 sprigs flat-leaf parsley, chopped

½ teaspoon extra virgin olive oil

Coarse salt

Remove and discard the radish greens. Grate the radishes on the large holes of a box grater and place in a medium bowl. Add the chopped olives and parsley and toss with the olive oil and a pinch of salt. Cover and refrigerate until ready to use.

 *continued on page 60*

FOR THE LEMON AND MINT SALAD

1 small lemon	¼ cup chopped fresh mint leaves
½ jalapeño pepper, stemmed, seeded, and minced	1 teaspoon extra virgin olive oil

Cut 3 very thin slices of lemon, then cut each slice into small wedges shaped like slices of pizza. Remove any seeds.

In a small bowl, toss the lemon wedges, jalapeño, mint leaves, and olive oil until the mint leaves are evenly coated with oil. Cover and refrigerate until ready to use.

FOR SERVING

1 pound sashimi-grade ahi tuna	Extra virgin olive oil
Coarse salt	

Arrange a mound of each salad on 4 large plates, dividing the salads evenly. Slice the tuna into thin strips and arrange several strips artfully over each salad. Garnish the fennel-based salad with 1 or 2 orange segments. Garnish the other two salads with a pinch of salt. If desired, drizzle all three salads with a bit more olive oil.

Prosciutto with Port-Marinated Figs and Gorgonzola Dolce

An enticing blend of salty, sweet, creamy, crunchy, earthy tastes and textures marks this marvelous opening dish. Salt-cured prosciutto is sweet and salty in its own right, while Gorgonzola dolce is the creamiest version of this well-known Italian blue cheese. Remember to bring it to room temperature or it will not be soft enough. The ensemble is highlighted by a bright, peppery edge and a lush Port wine sauce. MAKES 4 FIRST COURSE SERVINGS

AND IN YOUR GLASS

THIS STARTER CAN PAIR WITH MANY KINDS OF WINE, FROM LIGHTER WHITES SUCH AS SAUVIGNON BLANC OR PINOT GRIGIO TO RICHER BARREL-FERMENTED CHARDONNAY. SPARKLING WINE WOULD ALSO WORK WELL HERE, AS WOULD FRUITY RIESLING OR GEWÜRZTRAMINER— POSSIBLY YOUR BEST CHOICES.

2 tablespoons Port wine

2 tablespoons honey

2 teaspoons finely ground pepper

12 ripe Black Mission figs, halved lengthwise

¼ pound prosciutto, thinly sliced

4 ounces Gorgonzola dolce, at room temperature

¼ cup walnuts, halved and toasted (page 192)

Watercress or arugula, for garnish

In a medium bowl, combine the Port, honey, and pepper. Toss the figs in the marinade and leave them sitting, cut side down, at room temperature for 2 to 3 hours.

Lay out 2 or 3 slices of prosciutto on each of 4 salad plates. Arrange 6 fig halves cut side up in a circle on top of the prosciutto. Top each fig with a small dollop of the cheese. Place a walnut half on top of the cheese. Drizzle a small amount of the wine marinade over the walnuts. Garnish each plate with watercress or arugula.

Grilled Portobello Mushroom Sandwich on Focaccia with Eggplant, Red Peppers, and Sun-Dried Tomato/Goat Cheese Spread

With its meaty overtones and smoky, grilled nuances, this colorful sandwich will satisfy both vegetarians and carnivores alike. It's a perfect warm-weather treat, when al fresco grilling is at its peak. Or try it with any of the soups in this section for a heartwarming winter lunch. A full sandwich may be too substantial to be considered a first course, so if you are planning to serve this as a starter, cut it into quarters.

The mushrooms, eggplant, and peppers all require grilling. (If a grill is not an option, an oven broiler will also suffice.) But because these sandwich ingredients don't need to be eaten hot, we suggest you prepare them in advance at a pace that suits your needs. Focaccia bread (page 84), always a favorite with the PlumpJack chefs, is easy to make. But don't be shy about purchasing one from your local baker, either. A fresh, chewy ciabatta roll or other country bread can also substitute. MAKES 4 SANDWICHES, OR 8 FIRST COURSE SERVINGS

And in Your Glass

WINE MATCHES COULD INCLUDE SPICY WHITES LIKE GEWÜRZTRAMINER OR STEELY SAUVIGNON BLANC. A DRY ROSÉ WOULD DO THE JOB. AND EARTHY SYRAH OR PINOT NOIR WOULD SERVE WELL AS RED-WINE PAIRINGS. OR TRY A SPARKLING WINE— THE PERFECT APERITIF THAT GOES WITH JUST ABOUT ANYTHING.

1 small eggplant, cut into thin rounds

Coarse salt

½ cup sun-dried tomatoes

2 cloves garlic, minced

1 tablespoon balsamic vinegar

4 tablespoons extra virgin olive oil, plus oil for drizzling

4 large portobello mushrooms, stemmed

2 red bell peppers

1 tablespoon sherry vinegar

4 ounces soft, mild goat cheese

4 focaccia squares (5 inches), homemade (page 84) or commercial (see headnote)

1 to 2 ounces baby lettuce

Prepare an outdoor grill.

Sprinkle the eggplant rounds with salt and set aside for 30 minutes. Soak the sun-dried tomatoes in water for at least 30 minutes prior to using.

In a large bowl, whisk together the garlic, vinegar, 2 tablespoons of the olive oil, and a pinch of salt. Brush the tops of each mushroom with the oil mixture and brush (or spread with your fingers) the remaining oil onto the mushroom gills. Grill over a hot fire for 5 to 7 minutes per side, until the mushrooms are tender. Be careful not to let them burn. Set them aside.

continued on page 64

Roast the peppers on the grill, turning them until they are lightly blackened on all sides. Place the peppers in a bowl and cover it with plastic wrap to let them steam for 5 minutes. Remove the peppers from the bowl and peel off the skins under cool running water. Using your hands, split the peppers in two. Remove and discard the seeds and stems. Pat the pepper halves dry with a paper towel, drizzle with olive oil, and grill them until they are soft, 2 to 3 minutes per side. Remove from the heat and reserve.

Use a paper towel to wipe the eggplant slices free of any liquid they have sweated. Drizzle with olive oil, spreading the oil with your hands or a brush to coat the slices evenly. Grill until tender, about 3 minutes per side. Remove the slices from the grill and reserve until they are cool enough to handle.

In a large bowl, whisk together the sherry vinegar and the remaining 2 tablespoons olive oil. Using your hands, gently toss the eggplant and the peppers in the vinaigrette to coat them fully. Set them aside.

In a small food processor or a blender, blend the sun-dried tomatoes with 2 to 4 tablespoons of their soaking water until you have a coarse puree. Use a fork to combine the goat cheese and 3 tablespoons of the tomato puree.

Split the focaccia squares in half to create sandwich buns and toast them lightly on the grill. Spread the goat cheese mixture on the cut sides. Layer a mushroom, half a roasted pepper, several eggplant slices, and one-quarter of the lettuce on the bottom half of each bun. Cover with the top half. Cut each sandwich in half or quarters depending on your need.

CURRIED CHICKEN AND SPINACH SALAD This refreshing salad blends tender baby spinach leaves with chewy chunks of chicken, fruit, and tangy blue cheese. It's accented with tropical flair that comes from coconut milk, curry powder, and lively lime juice. The creamy curry dressing is mild and neatly coats the chicken and crunchy apple. Pomegranate seeds add sweetness.

If you can't find pomegranate seeds, you can substitute dried cranberries with excellent results. Leftover roast chicken (page 135) works quite well here, eliminating the need to cook chicken breasts from scratch. MAKES 4 MAIN COURSE SERVINGS

AND IN YOUR GLASS

THIS SALAD IS FILLED WITH

FRESH FRUITY FLAVORS

THAT CALL FOR A CHILLED

FRUIT-DRIVEN WHITE WINE

SUCH AS RIESLING OR

CHENIN BLANC. A CRISP

SPARKLING WINE WOULD

ALSO DO NICELY.

2 tablespoons extra virgin olive oil

1 pound boneless, skinless chicken breasts or 2 cups leftover cooked diced chicken (white or dark meat, skin removed)

Coarse salt and freshly ground pepper

¼ cup heavy cream

¼ cup coconut milk

2 teaspoons curry powder

1 tablespoon honey

1 tablespoon fresh lime juice

8 ounces baby spinach leaves

1 Granny Smith apple, cored and diced

¼ cup pomegranate seeds or coarsely chopped dried cranberries

¼ cup crumbled blue cheese

If not using leftover chicken, preheat oven to 400°F.

Coat the bottom of a small baking pan with 1 tablespoon of the olive oil. Season the chicken breasts with salt and pepper to taste, then rub with the remaining 1 tablespoon olive oil. Place the chicken in the pan and bake until golden brown, 25 to 30 minutes. When the chicken is cool enough to handle, cut into ½-inch dice and reserve.

While the chicken is baking, prepare the dressing. In a medium saucepan, mix the cream, coconut milk, curry powder, honey, and lime juice. Slowly simmer over low heat, stirring occasionally, until it thickens enough to coat a spoon easily, about 10 minutes. Remove from the heat and let cool.

In a large bowl, toss the chicken, spinach, apple, and pomegranate seeds with the curried coconut milk dressing until all the ingredients are evenly coated. Season with salt and pepper to taste. If desired, add additional dressing to taste and toss again. Garnish with crumbled blue cheese and serve at once.

THE CARNEROS INN

The art of living finds a unique expression at The Carneros Inn, located at the southern edge of Napa Valley. This PlumpJack resort and spa offers guests the luxury of their own contemporary country cottage—complete with a private courtyard—nestled into the hills surrounding the Hilltop restaurant. Here, and at the Boon Fly Café located at the inn's entrance, diners will find a varied cuisine prepared to match the wines of the region.

The view from the Hilltop does not disappoint. Pinot Noir and Chardonnay vines stretch out to the horizon, bathed in sumptuous Carneros sunlight. In the early evening, shadows play on the leafy vine canopies, creating a sea of green and black stripes that washes over the hillsides. Neighboring vintners ride their horses among the grapevines in a dreamlike setting that in the Carneros region is no dream. It's real life.

With such a backdrop, the spa takes on a special focus. Indeed, the "menu" here reflects the Carneros *terroir*—those natural elements that give the region its identity. Massages, facials, body wraps, manicures, and pedicures all employ various oils and creams made with locally sourced products. A mineral wrap begins with a grapeseed scrub; an assortment of massage lotions includes a house specialty made with honeydew melon, carrot, and lemon juice. Minerals from the Napa soil also enhance treatments. They include the healing gem and stone massage—a full-body massage that uses aromatherapy and smooth volcanic stones that date back to the primordial tectonic history of the region long, long ago.

Visitors to The Carneros Inn spa will find pitchers of the most delightful water strategically laid out for guests to refresh themselves. Subtly enhanced with mint, lemon, orange, and sometimes cucumber, these drinks are not only satisfying to the palate but also eminently suited to good health. Pure spring water is, of course, the quintessential cleanser for our bodies. In addition, lemon, orange, and cucumber are all natural diuretics that help detoxify our systems.

You can easily keep a pitcher of any of these drinks in your refrigerator for all occasions.

CITRUS-AND-MINT WATER
Fill a clear glass pitcher with 1 quart of spring or filtered water. Add 1 lemon or orange, cut into thin rounds, and 4 or 5 sprigs of mint. Chill in the refrigerator for a half hour prior to serving.

CUCUMBER WATER
Fill a clear glass pitcher with 1 quart of spring or filtered water. Cut 1 small cucumber into thin slices and add to the water. Chill in the refrigerator for a half hour prior to serving.

Mushroom Pizza with Caramelized Onions and Smoked Mozzarella

Smoky mozzarella cheese frames earthy mushrooms and sweet onions in an equally sweet embrace. Between the crust and the namesake ingredients lies a refreshing basil/parsley/arugula pesto. This pizza is often enjoyed as an appetizer or snack with a glass of wine at the bar at PlumpJack Cafe Squaw Valley. But it's substantial enough to serve as a main course preceded or accompanied by a salad, such as Baby Greens with Lemon Vinaigrette (page 50).

Your choice of mushroom here is important, but not critical. Look for buttery chanterelles and earthy hedgehogs when they are in season. Oyster mushrooms or the ubiquitous creminis will also add their own special flavors. A blend of two or three different mushrooms makes this pizza most interesting.

You can make your own pizza crust from scratch, but it's also okay to order ready-made dough from your neighborhood pizzeria. That will shave a lot of time off the preparation. MAKES 6 MAIN COURSE SERVINGS OR 8 TO 10 FIRST COURSE SERVINGS

AND IN YOUR GLASS

BECAUSE THIS PIZZA SERVES UP SO MANY DIFFERENT FLAVORS— FROM THE SWEET ONIONS TO THE EARTHY MUSHROOMS AND HERBAL PESTO—IT'S A CLASSIC CANDIDATE FOR MANY DIVERSE, YET COMPLEMENTARY, WINE PAIRINGS. SWEET LOVES FRUIT, AND FRUITY WHITE GEWÜRZTRAMINER, RIESLING, AND CHARDONNAY ARE ALL EXCELLENT WINE CHOICES. HERBAL SAUVIGNON BLANC WOULD ALSO MAKE A FINE MATCH. EARTHY RED SYRAH—OR EVEN A SYRAH ROSÉ— WOULD ALSO BE TEMPTING TO TRY. AMONG FRUIT-DRIVEN REDS, THINK PINOT NOIR OR ZINFANDEL.

FOR THE PESTO

5 cloves garlic confit (page 190)

1 cup extra virgin olive oil

½ cup firmly packed fresh flat-leaf parsley leaves

½ cup firmly packed fresh arugula leaves

1 cup firmly packed fresh basil leaves

Purée all the above ingredients in a blender or food processor and reserve.

FOR THE ONIONS

3 tablespoons extra virgin olive oil

3 medium onions, sliced

In a saucepan or heavy skillet, heat the olive oil over medium heat until it moves easily in the pan. Add the onions and stir to coat evenly with the oil. Reduce the heat to low and cook for about 1 hour, stirring every 10 minutes, until the onions are soft and slightly browned. Add more oil if necessary to prevent burning.

FOR THE PIZZA

2 tablespoons extra virgin olive oil

2 pounds mixed mushrooms, sliced (see headnote)

Basic pizza dough (page 199) or commercial dough

½ pound mozzarella cheese, freshly grated (about 2½ cups)

½ pound smoked mozzarella cheese, freshly grated (about 2½ cups)

Preheat oven to 500°F.

In a large, heavy skillet, heat the olive oil over high heat until it shimmers. Add the mushrooms, stir to coat with the oil, and sauté until soft, about 3 minutes. Set aside.

Lightly flour a work surface. Cut the dough into 2 equal pieces. Using a rolling pin, roll out each half of the dough to fit a 12- or 14-inch nonstick pizza pan or a 9-by-13-inch nonstick baking sheet. (If you don't have nonstick pans, use a tablespoon of olive or canola oil to coat each pan's surface.) Use additional flour as needed to prevent the dough from sticking. Transfer the dough to the pans and make a raised edge with your thumbs.

Thinly spread out the pesto to cover each pizza. Spread the onions evenly over the pesto. Evenly distribute the mozzarella and smoked mozzarella over each pie. Do the same with the sautéed mushrooms.

Bake until the edge of the crust is golden brown, 12 to 15 minutes.

Chicken Liver Flan Crème Caramel with Apple "Caviar"

Chicken Liver Flan Crème Caramel with Apple "Caviar" We usually think of crème caramel as dessert. Indeed, this creamy-smooth, light-textured, yet somehow lush appetizer visually resembles the sweet crème caramel we enjoy at the end of dinner. But this unusually original incarnation has a distinctly savory character, despite the syrup and apple influences. As garnish, a light apple "caviar" provides a welcome contrast to the rich liver custard, while caramelized syrup graces the dish as a classic topping. The PlumpJack chefs often use duck liver, but chicken livers are easier to find at your local grocer. They make a very fine flan, too.

For entertaining, you can prepare the flans in advance and refrigerate them, covered, for up to three days in their ramekins. The apple caviar also stores well in an airtight plastic container. To best highlight the velvety texture and subtle flavors, though, serve at room temperature. MAKES 4 FIRST COURSE SERVINGS

AND IN YOUR GLASS

ENJOY WITH AN "OFF-DRY"
OR SEMISWEET RIESLING
OR GEWÜRZTRAMINER.
RICH, BUTTERY
CHARDONNAY OR A
REFRESHING DRY ROSÉ
WILL ALSO WORK WELL IN
YOUR GLASS.

½ cup plus 2 tablespoons sugar

¼ cup water

2 Granny Smith apples, peeled, cored, and cut into tiny dice

1 tablespoon apple cider vinegar

1 tablespoon unsalted butter

3 chicken livers, trimmed (about 4 ounces total weight)

2 tablespoons dry sherry, such as amontillado

1 cup heavy cream

3 egg yolks

⅛ teaspoon freshly grated nutmeg

½ teaspoon coarse salt

Preheat oven to 300°F.

In a small saucepan, heat the ½ cup sugar and the water over high heat, stirring occasionally, until a thick, golden brown syrup forms, about 15 minutes. Immediately (before it begins to harden) pour the syrup into four 3-inch-wide ovenproof ramekins, dividing it equally. Set the ramekins aside.

Place the apple pieces into a nonstick pan, and stir in the remaining 2 tablespoons sugar and the cider vinegar. Cook over medium heat until the apple is tender, stirring occasionally, about 10 minutes. Remove from the heat and reserve in a nonreactive bowl or plastic container.

In a medium skillet, melt the butter over medium heat. Add the livers and cook until medium-rare, 2 to 3 minutes per side. Transfer the livers to a blender. Add the sherry to the skillet and stir to scrape up any browned bits from the bottom. Pour the sherry and liver juices

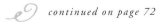 *continued on page 72*

into the blender. Add the cream, egg yolks, nutmeg, and salt and pulse until smooth and fairly liquid. Strain into a bowl through a fine-mesh sieve and discard the remaining solids.

Pour the liver mixture into the ramekins and set them in a baking pan filled halfway with hot water. Cover the pan with aluminum foil and crimp the foil loosely around the two shorter edges of the pan. Bake until the flans are set and firm, about 45 minutes. Remove from the oven, set the ramekins on a wire rack, and let cool to room temperature.

To remove the flans from the ramekins, run a paring knife around the edge of the custard. Place a small serving plate over the top of each ramekin. Hold it in place with one hand and flip the ramekin upside down. Gently tap the underside of the ramekin a few times and lift it off the molded custard.

Serve garnished with the apple caviar on the side.

Beef Carpaccio with Lemon Aioli, Truffle Oil, and Asparagus Salad

Tangy lemon and capers highlight the soft texture of raw beef, dressed with a dollop of aioli, a garlic-infused mayonnaise. Truffle oil, which can be found in most specialty grocery stores, is quite powerful. Cover most of the bottle opening with your thumb before pouring to allow only a limited number of drops per serving. **MAKES 4 FIRST COURSE SERVINGS**

FOR THE AIOLI

1 egg yolk, at room temperature	⅔ cup canola oil
2 teaspoons Dijon mustard	1 clove garlic, minced
Pinch of coarse salt	1 tablespoon grated lemon zest
½ cup extra virgin olive oil	2 teaspoons fresh lemon juice

In a bowl, combine the egg yolk, mustard, and salt and whisk to blend. Whisk in the oils, a very small amount at a time, until an emulsified sauce forms. (Or, in a food processor, pulse the egg yolk, mustard, and salt to combine. With the machine running, add the oils in a fine, steady stream, processing until an emulsified sauce forms.) Stir the garlic and lemon zest into the mayonnaise, mixing well. Whisk in the lemon juice and refrigerate until ready to use.

Refrigerate any extra aioli for up to 3 days to use as a dipping sauce or sandwich spread. (Makes about 1½ cups.)

FOR THE ASPARAGUS SALAD

½ pound asparagus, tough ends trimmed	Juice of ½ lemon
	1 tablespoon extra virgin olive oil
¼ cup coarsely chopped fresh flat-leaf parsley	Coarse salt and freshly ground pepper

Fill a large sauté pan with water to a depth of 1 inch and bring to a boil over high heat. Lay the asparagus in the water, cover, and cook until tender, 3 to 5 minutes. Drain in a colander and rinse immediately with very cold water to retain the color and stop the cooking.

Pat the asparagus dry with paper towels. Slice each spear into 1-inch lengths.

In a bowl, toss the asparagus with the parsley, lemon juice, and olive oil. Season with salt and pepper to taste.

 *continued on page 74*

FOR THE CARPACCIO

¼ pound beef tenderloin, cut into 4 medallions, each about ¼ inch thick

Coarse salt and freshly ground pepper

2 tablespoons caper berries

4 ounces Parmesan cheese

Truffle oil

Place 1 beef medallion between 2 sheets of plastic wrap. Using a meat mallet or the side of a meat cleaver, pound the medallion into a very thin, flat pancake 6 to 8 inches in diameter. (Be careful not to pound holes in the meat.) Lift off the top piece of plastic, flip the beef onto the center of a dinner plate, and peel off the second piece of plastic. Repeat with the remaining 3 medallions.

Season each slice of beef lightly with salt and pepper. Place a dollop of the aioli in the middle of each slice. Divide the caper berries equally to garnish each slice. Top with 4 or 5 thin shavings of Parmesan cheese and sprinkle sparingly with the truffle oil.

Place a small mound of the asparagus salad at one side of the carpaccio.

Salad and Wine

It's not salad that has given this pairing a bad name. The culprit lies in the vinegar that is used in so many salad dressings—aptly referred to as vinaigrettes. Vinegar is essentially spoiled wine, altered by the action of select bacteria. And while we wouldn't want to drink a bottle of vinegar, in small doses vinegar's intensely tangy acidity provides balance to what would otherwise be an overly oily salad dressing. Unfortunately, that tangy acidity can compete with a wine and give your dinner beverage a slightly "off" flavor.

Higher-acid wines, such as bubblies, whites, and rosés, can stand up to vinaigrette better than lower-acid reds. But that hasn't stopped countless generations of French and Italians from enjoying their mealtime wine—be it red or white—with the salad course. They just drink right through it. And you should, too.

If you intend to enjoy a truly great wine with your meal, serve the wine before or after the salad. But in most instances, just remember that a few sips of your wine might be slightly challenged during the salad course. A lower expectation at this juncture of your meal will actually raise your level of overall enjoyment.

Purists can mitigate the problem by making a vinegar-free vinaigrette using lemon or other citrus juices. But even with these nonvinegar vinaigrettes, pronounced acidity will still compromise most red wines.

ASPARAGUS SOUP This silky soup is enhanced by a crunchy radish garnish and a refreshing touch of mint. MAKES 6 SERVINGS

8 tablespoons (1 stick) unsalted butter	1 cup diced radishes
½ cup diced onion	1 tablespoon finely chopped fresh mint
1 large russet potato, peeled and diced	1 tablespoon extra virgin olive oil
1 tablespoon plus ¼ teaspoon coarse salt	2 pounds asparagus, tough ends trimmed
1 tablespoon sugar	¼ cup heavy cream
½ cup dry white wine	Pinch of freshly grated nutmeg
2 quarts water	Freshly ground pepper

AND IN YOUR GLASS

ENJOY A CHILLED GLASS
OF SPARKLING WINE OR
CRISP SAUVIGNON BLANC.

In a large soup pot, melt the butter over medium heat until it turns golden brown. Add the onion, potato, 1 tablespoon salt, and sugar and cook, stirring regularly, for 5 minutes, until the onion is translucent. Add the wine and water, increase the heat to high, and bring to a boil. Reduce the heat to simmer for 10 minutes.

While the soup is simmering, combine the radishes, mint, olive oil, and the remaining ¼ teaspoon salt in a small bowl. Set aside.

Fill a sauté pan with water to a depth of 1 inch and bring to a boil over high heat. Trim the tips off the asparagus and add them to the boiling water (reserve the stalks). Cover and cook the tips until tender, about 3 minutes. Drain in a colander and rinse immediately with cold water to retain the color and stop the cooking. Set aside.

Cut the asparagus stalks into 2-inch lengths and add them to the soup base, which should be done or nearly done simmering by now. Return to a simmer or continue to simmer for an additional 3 minutes.

Remove the soup from the heat and puree in a blender in small batches, being careful not to splatter the hot liquid. Transfer each batch of pureed liquid into a clean soup pot. When all the soup has been pureed, stir in the cream and add the nutmeg and the pepper to taste. Gently heat the soup until it simmers.

Serve in individual soup bowls. Garnish each serving with the radish/mint mixture and cooked asparagus tips.

TORTILLA SOUP This rich soup blends just a hint of heat with the seductive flavors of Mexico. Corn is the theme here, with corn tortillas giving the soup both body and texture. Fresh tomatoes give color and a sweet-edged brightness, while cilantro—found in many Mexican dishes—lends its distinctive herbaceous note.

MAKES 4 SERVINGS

2 tablespoons plus ⅓ cup extra virgin olive oil	6 cups diced ripe tomatoes (about 3 pounds)
1 onion, coarsely chopped	1 cup coarsely chopped fresh cilantro
3 cloves garlic, minced	2 cups chicken stock (page 194) or canned low-sodium chicken broth
¼ teaspoon cayenne pepper	Coarse salt and freshly ground pepper
9 corn tortillas (about 7 inches in diameter)	

AND IN YOUR GLASS

WHETHER IN LIQUID OR SOLID FORM, CORN TORTILLAS PAIR QUITE WELL WITH BEER. CREAMY CHARDONNAY WOULD ALSO BE A GOOD PARTNER.

In a large soup pot, heat the 2 tablespoons olive oil over medium heat until it moves easily in the pot. Cook the onion, garlic, and cayenne until the onion is translucent, about 3 minutes. Cut 6 of the tortillas into roughly 2-inch square pieces. Stir the pieces into the pan and cook for 30 seconds. Add the tomatoes, cilantro, chicken stock, and 1 teaspoon salt and stir well. Bring to a boil, reduce to simmer, cover, and cook for 45 minutes.

In a blender or food processor, puree the soup in batches until it is fairly smooth-textured. If desired, season with additional salt and pepper. Return the soup to the pot and reheat prior to serving.

Cut the remaining 3 tortillas into 3-inch-long, ¼-inch-wide strips. In a medium sauté pan, heat the ⅓ cup olive oil over medium-high heat until it shimmers. Fry the tortilla strips until they are crisp, about 2 minutes. Use a slotted spoon to remove them from the pan and drain on paper towels. Pat the tops of the tortilla strips dry with paper towel as well.

Pour the hot soup into soup bowls and garnish each serving with fried tortilla strips.

GAZPACHO Cool and refreshing, gazpacho is the perfect summertime soup. Best made with ultra-ripe tomatoes picked fresh from the vine, this soup serves up a tangy garlic edge emboldened by a touch of jalapeño pepper. Fresh cilantro gives it an exotic touch, with crunchy onion and cucumber offering a diversity of texture for the palate. MAKES 6 SERVINGS

1½ pounds very ripe tomatoes

4 cups water

2 cups cubed (2 inches) baguette or other country bread

2 tablespoons sherry vinegar

½ cup extra virgin olive oil

3 cloves garlic, minced

3 tablespoons minced red onion

1 small cucumber, peeled and diced

1 tablespoon minced fresh cilantro

1 jalapeño pepper, seeded and minced

1 tablespoon coarse salt

AND IN YOUR GLASS

ENJOY THIS WITH THE
PERFECT SUMMERTIME
WINE: DRY ROSÉ. CRISP
AND REFRESHING, ROSÉ
ALSO SERVES UP HINTS OF
RED FRUIT THAT PAIR
BEAUTIFULLY WITH RIPE
TOMATOES AND THE
SUBTLE SPICE OF
JALAPEÑO PEPPER.

Bring a large pot three-quarters full of water to a boil. With a paring knife, cut a shallow X in the blossom end of each tomato. Add the tomatoes, but be careful not to fill the pot to overflowing. After 30 to 40 seconds, use a slotted spoon to transfer the tomatoes to a bowl, then let cool for a minute or two. Starting with the X on each tomato, peel off the skin, then cut out and discard the shallow core from the stem end.

Puree the tomatoes with 3 cups of the water in a blender or food processor. (Puree in batches if necessary.) Transfer the tomato puree to a large bowl.

In a medium bowl, soak the bread in ½ of the cup water until it is fully moist, about 2 minutes. Puree the bread with the remaining ½ cup water in a blender or food processor. Stir the bread puree into the tomato puree. Gently stir in the vinegar, olive oil, garlic, onion, cucumber, cilantro, jalapeño, and salt until all the ingredients are mixed well.

Refrigerate for 2 hours prior to serving.

Udon Noodles in Hot and Sour Broth

Udon Noodles in Hot and Sour Broth Silky-smooth Japanese udon—or wheat—noodles and tofu find a welcome contrast in the crunchy wood ear mushrooms and toasted sesame seeds that also grace the broth. The chile oil gives off mild heat that warms the body from the inside out. This tangy, spicy dish is a perfect midwinter warm-up for blustery cold days by the San Francisco Bay or as a lunch break on the snowy ski slopes at Squaw Valley. MAKES 4 SERVINGS

AND IN YOUR GLASS

TRY SIPPING A CITRUSY

SAUVIGNON BLANC TO

REFRESH THE PALATE

AFTER A FEW SPOONFULS

OF THIS SATISFYING SOUP.

1 ounce dried wood ear mushrooms (see note below)

1 ounce dried shiitake mushrooms

½ pound dried udon noodles (see note below)

1 tablespoon toasted sesame oil

1 large carrot, thinly sliced

¼ cup canned sliced water chestnuts

1 teaspoon chile sesame oil

½ pound firm tofu, cut into 1-inch cubes

5 cups chicken stock (page 194) or canned low-sodium vegetable or chicken broth

⅓ cup rice wine vinegar

¼ cup tamari or soy sauce

2 tablespoons unsalted butter, cut into 4 pieces

3 scallions (white part only), sliced in thin rounds

¼ cup loosely packed chopped fresh cilantro

2 tablespoons toasted sesame seeds (page 192)

1 lime, quartered

Combine the wood ears and shiitake in a large bowl and cover with hot water. Soak for about 20 minutes to reconstitute them. Drain and discard the liquid. Reserve the mushrooms.

Bring a medium saucepan of water to a boil over high heat. Add the udon noodles. When the water begins to boil again, reduce the heat to medium and cook until the noodles are tender, about 4 minutes. Drain in a colander and reserve.

In a large sauté pan, heat the toasted sesame oil over medium heat until it moves easily across the pan. Add the mushrooms, carrot, and chestnuts and cook until the carrot is soft, about 10 minutes. Add the chile oil. Gently stir in the tofu and continue to cook for 1 minute.

Meanwhile, in a large soup pot, bring the stock, rice wine vinegar, and soy sauce to a boil. Reduce the heat to simmer. While the broth is simmering, divide the noodles evenly among 4 large soup bowls. Top each portion of noodles with a pat of the butter and one-quarter of the mushroom mixture. Ladle the hot broth over the noodles and vegetables. Garnish each serving with the scallions, cilantro, sesame seeds, and the juice of 1 lime wedge. Serve piping hot.

Note: Look for dried wood ear mushrooms and udon noodles in the Asian foods section of your supermarket.

Butternut Squash Soup with Fresh Sage

This rustic soup delivers immense satisfaction with just a small number of simple ingredients. The key is fresh sage, which adds an intriguing herbal note to the sweet butternut squash. MAKES 4 TO 6 SERVINGS

1 large or 2 small butternut squash (about 3 pounds total weight)

1½ tablespoons unsalted butter

10 to 12 sprigs sage

1 cup diced onion

3 cloves garlic, coarsely chopped

1 large white or Yukon Gold potato (6 to 7 ounces), scrubbed and diced

¼ teaspoon freshly grated nutmeg

6 cups chicken stock (page 194) or canned low-sodium chicken broth

Coarse salt and freshly ground pepper

AND IN YOUR GLASS
ENJOY AS A FIRST COURSE
IN FALL WITH A GLASS OF
CHILLED FRUITY RIESLING
OR GEWÜRZTRAMINER OR
A LUSH, BUTTERY
CHARDONNAY.

Preheat oven to 350°F.

Halve the squash lengthwise, remove the seeds, and rub both halves with ½ tablespoon butter. Place a sprig of sage in each squash cavity. Place the squash cut side up in a roasting pan and bake until the flesh begins to soften, 45 to 60 minutes. Remove from the oven, discard the sage, and let the squash sit until cool enough to handle with your bare hands.

When the squash has nearly finished roasting, melt the remaining 1 tablespoon butter in a large soup pot over medium heat. Add the onion and garlic and cook, stirring occasionally, until the onion becomes translucent, about 3 minutes. Add the potato and cook for another minute, stirring occasionally.

Remove the leaves from the remaining sage sprigs. Discard the stems. Chop the leaves coarsely. (They should fill approximately ½ cup, loosely packed.) Stir the leaves into the pot. Stir in the nutmeg. Add the chicken stock, bring to a boil, and reduce to simmer.

Spoon out the flesh from the squash and chop it coarsely. Add the squash to the simmering soup and cook for 15 more minutes.

Remove the pot from the heat and let the soup cool briefly. Pulse the soup in batches in a food processor to make a coarse puree and transfer to a clean pot. (Try not to overpulse; the soup should retain small bits of squash, potato, and sage.)

Add salt to taste and reheat prior to serving if necessary. Ladle into soup bowls and garnish with freshly ground pepper to taste.

VERSATILE SIDES

Side dishes don't have to be eaten on the side. The Oven-Roasted Brussels Sprouts on page 88 makes a fine first course without any other trappings. Gnocchi (page 94)—with the right sauce—is substantial enough to serve as a main course. So is the Butternut Squash, Potato, and Oyster Mushroom Gratin on page 93.

Many of the following side dishes are recommended with at least one recipe found later in this book. But feel free to enjoy them outside the parameters suggested here. Both Sautéed Kale (page 86) and Braised Red Cabbage (page 90) bring fresh flavors to many meat- or fish-based meals inspired by Mediterranean, Asian, or Central American cooking. Skins-On Mashed Potatoes (page 92) and Oven-Roasted Potato "Fries" (page 91) add savory substance to a broad range of dishes. Indeed, the sides that follow pair up easily with an endless array of main courses from almost any culinary repertoire.

Focaccia Bread with Fresh Rosemary

Toasty focaccia is great for dipping in extra virgin olive oil or as a bread accompaniment to any meal. It's perfect with the soups and salads featured in this book. At PlumpJack's Napa Valley Boon Fly Café, focaccia is the bread of choice for the Grilled Portobello Mushroom Sandwich (page 62). Rosemary grows in profusion in Napa, and it's easy to pick a few sprigs to use for garnish there. But any kind of herb—fresh or dried—will enhance this rustic bread.

Texture is important. The best country breads use a portion of high-gluten flour, milled from hard wheat. It gives a slightly chewier feel than the softer crumb of cakes and muffins, typically made with flours blended from hard and soft wheat. You can find high-gluten flour, sometimes called "gluten" or simply "bread flour," in the baking section of most supermarkets.

Remember that you'll need to let the dough rise twice—once for at least an hour, and again for a half hour—prior to baking. MAKES 1 LOAF, 10 BY 15 INCHES

1 envelope (2¼ teaspoons) active dry yeast	2 cups unbleached all-purpose flour, plus more for kneading and rolling
1¼ cups warm water	½ teaspoon coarse salt, plus coarse sea salt for garnish
3 tablespoons extra virgin olive oil, plus more for garnish	2 tablespoons chopped fresh rosemary
½ cup high-gluten flour	

In a large bowl, combine the yeast with 1 cup of the warm water. Let rest for 10 minutes, until slightly foamy. Stir in the 3 tablespoons olive oil. Using a wooden spoon, stir in the high-gluten flour. Add the 2 cups all-purpose flour and ½ teaspoon salt. Stir with the wooden spoon until a sticky dough begins to form. Add the remaining ¼ cup warm water and use your hands to shape the dough into a large ball.

Dust your hands with a little all-purpose flour and knead the dough in the bowl, pushing it down with the heel of your hand, then pulling it together in a mound. Repeat this until the dough becomes elastic, 4 to 5 minutes.

Lightly oil another large bowl. Place the dough in the bowl, cover it with plastic wrap or a damp dish towel, and leave it in a warm place (about 70°F) to rise until it has doubled in size, at least 1 hour. (Cooler temperatures will slow down the rising process.)

Lightly flour your work surface. Remove the risen dough from the bowl, roll it in additional flour to keep it from sticking, punch it down, and knead it for a few more minutes. Then slowly stretch the dough to a rectangular shape about 15 inches long and 10 inches wide. Lightly oil a 10-by-15-inch baking pan and place the dough in the pan. Cover it with plastic wrap and let it rise for 30 minutes.

About 10 minutes before the focaccia has finished rising, preheat the oven to 400°F.

Uncover the dough and press little dimples across the top with your index finger. Sprinkle the surface with the rosemary, drizzle with a little more olive oil, and garnish with a pinch or two of coarse sea salt. Set in the oven and bake until golden brown, about 30 minutes.

SAUTÉED KALE WITH GARLIC

Sautéing kale in olive oil with garlic reveals both sweetness and softness in this vitamin-rich vegetable. Kale can serve admirably as a side for many main dishes, particularly Mustard and Meyer Lemon Pork Tenderloin with Dry Jack Polenta (page 148). Using this same recipe, you can easily substitute other fibrous, leafy greens such as Swiss chard or bok choy. MAKES 4 OR 5 SIDE DISH OR FIRST COURSE SERVINGS

3 tablespoons extra virgin olive oil

3 cloves garlic, minced

1 pound kale, coarsely chopped

3 tablespoons water

Coarse salt and freshly ground pepper

In a large sauté pan or Dutch oven, heat the olive oil over medium-high heat until it shimmers. Add the garlic and stir until it has browned slightly, about 30 seconds. Add the kale and toss until the leaves are coated with the oil.

Add the water and stir to break up any bits of garlic that may have stuck to the pan. Cover and simmer, stirring occasionally, until the leaves are tender, 5 to 7 minutes. To prevent searing, add another tablespoon or two of water if the liquid evaporates before the kale has cooked. When the kale is done, remove from the heat, season with salt and pepper, toss again, and cover to keep warm until ready to serve.

BAKED BROCCOLI FLORETS This rustic preparation is quite satisfying in its simplicity. Baked with only butter, salt, and pepper, these broccoli florets reveal a purity of flavor highlighted by a hint of smokiness and just a wisp of crunchiness on the otherwise soft, flowery part of the vegetable. MAKES 4 TO 6 SIDE DISH SERVINGS

1 bunch broccoli (about 2 pounds)	2 tablespoons unsalted butter
Coarse salt	Freshly ground pepper

Preheat oven to 450°F.

Trim and discard the tough ends of the broccoli. Reserve the florets and about 2 inches of their stems.

Fill a medium pot halfway with lightly salted water and bring to a boil. Add the broccoli, bring the water back to a boil, and blanch the florets for 2 minutes. Remove with a slotted spoon and reserve.

Coat the surface of a large ovenproof skillet or pan with 1 tablespoon of the butter. Place the florets in the pan. Add salt and pepper to taste. Cut the remaining tablespoon butter into small pieces and dot the florets with them.

Bake until the broccoli is tender, 15 to 20 minutes.

Serve at once with additional butter and salt for garnish, if desired.

OVEN-ROASTED BRUSSELS SPROUTS WITH BACON Sweet,

earthy Brussels sprouts take on a slightly smoky flavor in the oven. Bacon builds
on that theme and frames the sprouts with a deliciously salty edge as well. Served
piping hot directly from the pan, these tiny cabbages will add depth of flavor to many
main dishes, from Smoked Salmon Frittata (page 38) to Seared Wild Salmon (page
118), Goose Breast with Red Wine Gravy (page 136), or Pork Chops with Sweet Corn
Maque Chaux (page 141). MAKES 4 TO 6 SIDE DISH SERVINGS

2 slices bacon, finely chopped	⅛ teaspoon coarse salt
2 tablespoons extra virgin olive oil	3 tablespoons water
½ medium onion, coarsely chopped	Freshly ground pepper
2 cloves garlic, minced	
2 pounds Brussels sprouts, trimmed and halved	

Preheat oven to 375°F.

In a large ovenproof skillet or pan, cook the bacon over medium-high heat, stirring
occasionally, until it starts to turn crisp, about 2 minutes. Add 1 tablespoon of the olive oil and
the onion and cook for 1 minute, stirring occasionally. Lower the heat to medium-low and stir
in the garlic. Cook for 1 more minute.

Add the Brussels sprouts, the remaining 1 tablespoon olive oil, and the salt. Gently stir to
coat the sprouts evenly with the oil and salt. Remove the pan from the heat and add the water.
Gently stir again and place the pan in the oven on the middle rack. Roast, stirring gently every
5 minutes, until the sprouts are golden brown and tender enough to be easily pierced with a
fork, about 20 minutes. Garnish with pepper and serve.

BRAISED RED CABBAGE WITH BACON

This tangy, spiced cabbage adds zip to a meal and works particularly well alongside sweet meats such as pork or, more specifically, the richly textured Goose Breast with Red Wine Gravy on page 136. Try it in tandem with Skins-On Mashed Potatoes (page 92) for a double-edged side dish special. MAKES 4 TO 6 SIDE DISH SERVINGS

5 slices bacon, cut into ¼-inch matchsticks	3 juniper berries
1 onion, diced	1½ teaspoons whole cloves, tied in a piece of cheesecloth
1 head red cabbage, shredded	1½ teaspoons coarse salt
⅓ cup cider vinegar	¼ teaspoon freshly ground pepper

In a large, deep skillet, cook the bacon and onion over high heat, stirring occasionally, until the bacon is crisp, about 5 minutes. Add the cabbage, vinegar, juniper berries, cloves, salt, and pepper. Stir and reduce the heat to medium. Simmer uncovered, stirring every 5 or 10 minutes, until the cabbage is wilted and soft, about 30 minutes. (Add ¼ cup water if the cabbage begins to dry out.)

When the cabbage is cooked through, remove the cloves. (The juniper berries are crunchy and edible.) Transfer to a serving bowl and serve at once.

Oven-Roasted Potato "Fries" with Rosemary and Extra Virgin Olive Oil

Unless you've got a commercial fryer, it's hard to make french fries at home the way they do at Balboa Cafe. The good news is that you can use your home oven to make a potato crisp that is just as tasty and perhaps healthier.

These crispy potato rounds feature the fragrance of roasted rosemary and fruity olive oil. They go well with everything from the Balboa Burger (page 152) to the Smoked Salmon Frittata (page 38), as well as just about any piece of grilled meat or fish. MAKES 4 OR 5 SIDE DISH SERVINGS

5 tablespoons extra virgin olive oil

3 pounds large white or Yukon Gold potatoes, scrubbed

1 tablespoon dried rosemary

Coarse salt and freshly ground pepper

Preheat oven to 400°F. Coat the bottom of a large roasting pan with 2 tablespoons of the olive oil.

Slice the potatoes into ⅛-inch-thick rounds. Arrange the slices in slightly overlapping rows to cover the bottom of the pan. Drizzle the remaining 3 tablespoons olive oil over the top, then sprinkle with the rosemary. Season with salt and pepper.

Bake the potatoes until golden brown, about 30 minutes. Serve at once or keep warm in the oven.

Skins-On Mashed Potatoes with Crème Fraîche
These smooth, creamy, soft spuds give true meaning to the phrase "comfort food" and pair well with any number of recipes throughout this book, particularly Seared Wild Salmon (page 118). They also play a role in the Braised Short Ribs Shepherd's Pie (page 161). Home cooks can revel in the fact that no peeling is required. MAKES 6 SIDE DISH SERVINGS

3 pounds white or Yukon Gold potatoes, scrubbed

4 tablespoons (½ stick) unsalted butter

½ cup heavy cream

½ cup crème fraîche

Coarse salt and freshly ground pepper

Cut the potatoes into 1½- to 2-inch chunks. Fill a large pot halfway to two-thirds with water and bring to a boil. Add the potatoes and cook over medium-high heat until they are tender, about 20 minutes. Drain in a colander and return the potatoes to the pot. Add the butter, cream, and crème fraîche. Mash with a hand masher until fairly smooth. Do not overmash, however. Small lumps are desirable. Season with salt and pepper to taste.

Butternut Squash, Potato, and Oyster Mushroom

Gratin This variation on the classic potato gratin features a crunchy top that contrasts with the lush, creamy interior. Potatoes play a pivotal role here, but they are supported by silky oyster mushrooms and sweet butternut squash, revealing a far more interesting taste sensation than a standard potato gratin. And in this gratin, the traditional cream is enhanced by fresh, soft goat cheese. Although it makes an excellent side, this dish can also serve well as a main course with cooked greens, such as kale, or a salad on the side.

Make sure you slice your potatoes and squash thin, or they will not cook completely. For best slicing results, use a large, sharp knife or—for greater ease—a food processor or mandoline. MAKES 4 MAIN COURSE SERVINGS OR 6 SIDE DISH SERVINGS

2 large eggs

½ pound mild, soft goat cheese, cut into small pieces or crumbled

3 tablespoons extra virgin olive oil

1 clove garlic, minced

2 shallots, diced

1 pound oyster (or other) mushrooms, rinsed and coarsely chopped

5 or 6 white potatoes, scrubbed and thinly sliced

Coarse salt

1 small butternut squash (about 1½ to 2 pounds), peeled, halved, seeded, and thinly sliced

3 cups heavy cream

Freshly ground pepper

Preheat oven to 350°F.

In a mixing bowl, beat the eggs and the goat cheese until smooth and thick. Set aside.

In a large skillet or sauté pan, heat 2 tablespoons of the olive oil over medium heat until the oil moves easily across the pan. Cook the garlic and the shallots until the garlic is golden and the shallots translucent, about 2 minutes. Add the mushrooms and cook until they soften, about 5 minutes.

Oil a 10-by-14-inch baking dish with the remaining 1 tablespoon olive oil. Lay half of the potato slices in an even layer on the bottom of the baking dish. Sprinkle a pinch or two of salt over the potatoes. Top with an even layer of half the squash. Spread half of the egg/goat cheese mixture over the squash. Top with a layer of half the sautéed mushrooms. Repeat the layers and pour the cream evenly over the top.

Bake until the potatoes and squash are tender, 50 to 55 minutes. Remove from the oven and let cool to allow the gratin to firm up before serving. Season with additional salt and freshly ground pepper to taste.

GNOCCHI WITH FRESH BASIL PESTO

GNOCCHI WITH FRESH BASIL PESTO Classic hearty potato dumplings—or gnocchi—are a staple of northern Italy. They make a fine starter, side, or main course and easily substitute for traditional wheat pastas. The pillow-like surface of light, fluffy gnocchi coats easily, carrying flavors along the palate in a satisfying and efficient manner.

These gnocchi are paired with fresh basil pesto. But you can also enjoy them with any favorite pasta sauce, or simply tossed with extra virgin olive oil and fresh herbs, then topped with grated Parmesan cheese.

Make the pesto sauce in advance for greatest ease in the kitchen. Fresh gnocchi can be stored for up to 24 hours, covered, in the refrigerator. MAKES 4 OR 5 MAIN COURSE SERVINGS OR 6 FIRST COURSE SERVINGS

FOR THE PESTO

1 cup extra virgin olive oil

4 cups firmly packed fresh basil leaves

2 tablespoons pine nuts (optional)

½ cup freshly grated Parmesan cheese

2 cloves garlic, minced

Coarse salt and freshly ground pepper

In a blender or food processor, combine ¼ cup of the olive oil and the basil leaves and puree, adding additional oil in ¼-cup increments, until smooth. Add the pine nuts, if using, and the Parmesan cheese and continue to blend until smooth. Add the garlic and pulse to incorporate. If the pesto is too thick, blend in a few additional tablespoons of olive oil. Season with salt and pepper. If not using right away, place in a sealed container and refrigerate for up to 3 days. (Makes about 2 cups.)

FOR THE GNOCCHI

3 russet potatoes (2 to 2½ pounds total weight)

1 large egg

⅓ cup sour cream

1 teaspoon coarse salt

1 cup all-purpose flour, plus more for kneading and dusting

Freshly ground pepper

Freshly grated Parmesan cheese, for serving

Preheat oven to 400°F.

Prick the skin of each potato with a fork. Bake for 1 hour or until the potatoes feel soft and the skins are firm. When they are cool enough to handle, halve the potatoes lengthwise. Spoon

continued on page 96

the potato flesh into a large bowl and discard the skins. Use a hand masher to mash the potatoes until they are smooth, with a light-textured, almost powdery consistency. Using a wooden spoon, thoroughly stir in the egg, sour cream, and salt. Stir in the 1 cup flour until a dough begins to form. When it is too thick to stir, use your hands and start kneading it.

When your hands become too sticky with dough, dust them with all-purpose flour. Continue kneading the dough in the bowl, pushing it down with the heel of your hand, then pulling it together in a mound. Repeat until the dough becomes supple and malleable, about 5 minutes.

Lightly flour a flat work surface. Place the dough on the surface and cut it into 8 to 10 pieces. Using the palm of your hand, roll each piece into a long, thin, sausage about 1 inch in diameter. Cut each length into small cylinders about 1 to 1½ inches long and gently roll the short cylinders in additional flour to coat them. This will keep them from sticking to each other and the work surface.

Bring a large pot of lightly salted water to a boil. For best results, cook the gnocchi in single-portion batches of 15 to 20 dumplings. As the gnocchi rise to the surface of the boiling water (1 to 2 minutes), use a slotted spoon to transfer them to a colander to drain.

Place each portion of gnocchi on a dinner plate and gently toss them with 2 or 3 tablespoons of the pesto. Season with salt and pepper to taste and garnish with freshly grated Parmesan cheese.

Wild Rice with Mushrooms and Toasted Pine Nuts

With its nutty, firm texture, wild rice (which isn't a true rice) makes a versatile and refreshing alternative to white rice. But like any grain, it can be somewhat plain on its own. Here, mushrooms and pine nuts add a complex, earthy sweetness. For a robust yet elegant year-end holiday meal, try this wild rice paired with Goose Breast with Red Wine Gravy (page 136). MAKES 4 TO 6 SIDE DISH SERVINGS

4 cups water

Coarse salt

1 cup wild rice

2 tablespoons extra virgin olive oil

½ cup minced onion

4 medium white button mushrooms, finely chopped

½ cup toasted pine nuts (page 192)

Freshly ground pepper

In a medium pot or saucepan, bring the water and ½ teaspoon salt and bring to a boil. Add the wild rice, bring to a boil again, reduce to simmer, and cover. Cook slowly until all or most of the water is absorbed, about 1 hour. The rice should be slightly al dente but also somewhat fluffy. (If water remains in the pot, drain the rice in a colander.) Cover and reserve.

In a large sauté pan or skillet, heat the olive oil over medium heat until it moves easily across the pan. Add the onion and cook until translucent, about 3 minutes. Add the mushrooms and stir gently to coat with the oil. Reduce the heat to medium-low, cover, and cook until the mushrooms have cooked through, about 10 minutes. (If the mushrooms start to sear, add 1 to 2 tablespoons water to the pan.)

Add the wild rice and pine nuts to the pan and toss to blend with the mushrooms and onions. Season to taste with salt and pepper and transfer to a large serving bowl.

SEAFOOD

San Francisco and its neighboring wine communities are strongly influenced by the Pacific Coast, where the cold, dark water has long provided sustenance for local dinner tables. The city is set on a peninsula, nearly surrounded by the sea. From Gold Rush days until the early twentieth century, Italian fishermen plied the bay in small green sailboats reminiscent of fishing vessels used for centuries in their native land. According to legend, they sang—sometimes arias from famous Italian operas—to identify themselves to other sailors shrouded in the fog that regularly blankets the water.

Today's commercial fishing craft range far and wide, blessed with modern-day radios and sonar to track each other and the diverse marine life swimming below the surface of the water. Fall and winter are the seasons for large, spiny Dungeness crabs. The sweet flesh of these crustaceans is eaten in many forms, including crab cakes (page 100). Wild salmon—native to these waters as well as the Pacific Northwest—also reside here. Each fall, they swim up from the sea and into the local rivers to spawn. These large copper-colored fish can be seen throughout the wine country as they wriggle through shallow streambeds before releasing their eggs.

Offshore kelp beds provide a kind of undersea forest home for a diverse population of sea creatures, most of which are celebrated in the local cuisine. Bay waters also harbor some of the West's best-known oyster farms, which provide a steady supply of fresh, briny bivalves, typically washed down with equally fresh chilled white and rosé wines.

Local wines also benefit from the marine topography in terms of viticulture. The ocean fog doesn't stop at the shoreline. It travels inland—usually in the early morning and late afternoon—creating a cooling phenomenon that makes California's coastal vineyards unique. Warm days and cool nights create a balance of ripeness and firm acidity in the grapes, characteristics that translate to lush fruit flavors and fine structure in the wines.

Ultimately, the San Francisco Bay area is a paradise for both fish and hungry humans. PlumpJack's chefs take advantage of this ocean bounty on a daily basis, serving up a dazzling array of seafood. Those dishes included here are among the most popular and often requested throughout the restaurant group.

CRAB CAKES WITH AVOCADO SALSA

CRAB CAKES WITH AVOCADO SALSA Each fall, San Franciscans await the annual Dungeness crab season with great anticipation. The sweet meat from these large, feisty crabs is perfect for a crab cake, and these substantial, full-bodied cakes are balanced with tangy avocado salsa and a squirt of fresh lemon juice.

If Dungeness crabs are unavailable, fresh lump crabmeat will suffice. Most fishmongers will sell you fresh crabmeat that has been picked from the shell, which saves a lot of time for the home cook. MAKES 4 MAIN COURSE SERVINGS OR 6 FIRST COURSE SERVINGS

FOR THE CRAB CAKES

3 to 4 ounces sea scallops

1 large egg

¼ teaspoon coarse salt

½ cup heavy cream

1 cup panko (see note on opposite page)

1 pound fresh Dungeness (or other) lump crabmeat, picked over

1 small ripe tomato, peeled (page 198) and finely chopped

2 tablespoons coarsely chopped fresh cilantro

4 tablespoons extra virgin olive oil

1 teaspoon Dijon mustard

2 tablespoons canola oil

AND IN YOUR GLASS

THESE CRAB CAKES TEAM UP NICELY WITH A GLASS OF BRIGHT SAUVIGNON BLANC, CREAMY CHARDONNAY, OR COOL, DRY ROSÉ.

Preheat oven to 350°F.

In a blender or food processor, pulse the scallops, egg, and salt until the mixture is thick and smooth. Add the cream and pulse again until it is blended well, but the mixture is still thick.

Transfer the scallop and cream mixture to a large mixing bowl. Using a wooden spoon, thoroughly stir in the panko. Add the crabmeat, tomato, cilantro, 2 tablespoons of the olive oil, and the mustard. Mix gently but thoroughly, using the spoon or your hands, trying not to break up the crabmeat. Divide the mixture into 4 or 6 balls (4 if you are serving the crab cakes as a main course, 6 for a first course). Shape the balls into patties about 1 inch thick.

In a large skillet, heat the remaining 2 tablespooons olive oil and the canola oil over medium heat until shimmering. Brown the crab cakes on both sides until golden, 3 to 4 minutes per side.

Transfer the cakes to a baking sheet and bake until firm, about 15 minutes.

While the crab cakes are baking, prepare the avocado salsa.

FOR THE SALSA

3 ripe avocados, pitted and peeled	2 teaspoons Champagne vinegar
1 cup water	½ teaspoon coarse salt
Juice of ½ lemon	Freshly ground pepper
½ cup loosely packed fresh cilantro	

Combine the avocados, water, lemon juice, cilantro, and vinegar in a blender. Pulse until smooth and creamy. Season with salt and pepper. Transfer the salsa to a small serving bowl.

TO SERVE

4 or 6 large butter lettuce leaves	1 lemon, cut into 4 or 6 wedges

Place a lettuce leaf on each plate and set a crab cake on top of it. Garnish with the avocado salsa and a lemon wedge.

Note: Panko, Japanese bread crumbs, are coarser in texture and stay crisp longer than ordinary bread crumbs. They make a lighter and flakier fry. Look for them in the Asian foods section of your supermarket or specialty store.

Brazilian Mussel Stew

A hint of spice and coconut highlights these briny, sweet mussels swimming deliciously in a fennel-infused broth. Think of this as a Brazilian take on French *moules marinière*.

If you want more heat, use the fiery habanero pepper. Otherwise, stick with milder serrano or jalapeño peppers. Either way, remember to wash your hands after handling them. Accidental rubbing of the eyes can be painful! Pay attention to the cooking time for these tasty bivalves. Cooked too long, they become tough and chewy.

Don't forget your soup spoon for the broth. MAKES 4 MAIN COURSE SERVINGS OR 8 FIRST COURSE SERVINGS

AND IN YOUR GLASS

THE BRINY SWEETNESS OF THIS DISH IS COMPLEMENTED BY A RICHLY STYLED WHITE WINE, LUSHLY TEXTURED BUT WITH FIRM ACIDITY. TRY BARREL-FERMENTED CHARDONNAY OR VIOGNIER FOR AN EXCELLENT PAIRING.

FOR THE BROTH

1 quart fish stock (page 193) or 4 bottles (8 ounces each) clam juice

1 bottle (750 ml) dry white wine

2 tomatoes, coarsely chopped

1 onion, diced

1 rib celery, coarsely chopped

2 tablespoons fennel seeds

1 habanero or 2 serrano or jalapeño peppers, halved and seeded

In a large pot, bring the fish stock, wine, tomatoes, onion, celery, fennel, and peppers to a boil. Reduce the heat to simmer for 1 hour. Strain the liquid through a sieve and transfer to a soup pot large enough to hold 4 pounds of mussels. Discard the solids.

FOR THE STEW

2 tablespoons peanut oil

6 plum tomatoes, cut into eighths

4 pounds fresh mussels, scrubbed and debearded

¼ cup roasted unsalted peanuts

2 cloves garlic confit (page 190) or roasted garlic (page 191)

1 cup coconut milk

½ bunch fresh cilantro leaves, chopped

Add the peanut oil and tomatoes to the broth and bring to a boil over medium-high heat. Add the mussels and stir them into the broth. Cover and cook, shaking the pan occasionally, until the shells are open, 2 to 3 minutes.

While the mussels are cooking, place the peanuts, garlic, and coconut milk in a blender. Pulse to blend.

Remove the mussels from the pot, dividing them among large soup bowls. Stir the peanut/coconut mixture into the broth and serve the mussels with plenty of broth. Garnish each bowl with cilantro.

Fish Tacos with Mango Salsa and Creamy Black Bean Salad

These tacos are finger food at its finest, and with the accompanying bean salad, they are admirably suited to a summer weekend lunch or dinner outdoors by the grill. Tangy mango salsa brings a fresh, fruity quality to these soft fish tacos; raw cabbage adds a crunchy accent. Use the freshest soft corn tortillas possible.

Prepare the salsa and bean salad first. They can wait at room temperature while you make the tacos. If using dried beans, remember to cook them well in advance, but last-minute cooks shouldn't be ashamed to use canned beans. Rice, too, needs to be cooked beforehand, although it doesn't require the forethought needed for dried beans.

Any meaty fish fillets will work well. Try halibut, salmon, or cod, for example. The fish can be simply grilled or broiled. MAKES 6 SERVINGS

AND IN YOUR GLASS

HOT DAYS AND A TOUCH OF CHILE ON THE PALATE REQUIRE COOL, REFRESHING WINES FOR BALANCE. TRY CHILLED DRY ROSÉ OR ANY FRUITY WHITE WINE AS AN ACCOMPANIMENT. A COLD BEER MIGHT DO THE TRICK WITH EQUAL APLOMB!

FOR THE SALSA

2 ripe mangos, peeled, seeded, and diced

½ cucumber, peeled and diced

1 ancho chile, seeded, stemmed, and diced

1 jalapeño pepper, seeded, stemmed, and minced

½ cup chopped fresh cilantro

Juice of 1 lime

¼ cup extra virgin olive oil

⅛ teaspoon coarse salt

In a large bowl, thoroughly mix the mangos, cucumber, ancho chile, jalapeño, cilantro, lime juice, olive oil, and salt. Set aside.

FOR THE BLACK BEAN SALAD

½ cup coconut milk (see note on page 106)

¼ cup plus 1 tablespoon extra virgin olive oil

Juice of 1 lime

½ cup chopped fresh cilantro

¼ teaspoon coarse salt

⅛ teaspoon cayenne pepper

2 medium onions, diced

2 carrots, cut into small dice

2 red bell peppers, seeded, stemmed, and diced

2 ancho chiles, seeded, stemmed, and diced

4 cups cooked black beans (page 200), or 2 cans, rinsed and drained (15 ounces each)

In a blender or food processor, blend the coconut milk, ¼ cup olive oil, lime juice, cilantro, salt, and cayenne. Set aside.

continued on page 106

In a sauté pan or skillet, heat the remaining 1 tablespoon olive oil over medium heat until it shimmers. Add the onions and cook until they are translucent, about 3 minutes. Add the carrots, red peppers, and chiles. Cook, stirring occasionally, until the carrots and peppers are moderately soft, about 5 minutes. Transfer to a large mixing bowl.

Add the beans to the vegetables. Stir in the coconut/cilantro sauce and set aside until ready to use. The bean salad can be eaten warm or at room temperature.

FOR THE TACOS

2 pounds meaty fish fillets, such as halibut, salmon, or cod, pin bones removed

Coarse salt and freshly ground pepper

1 tablespoon extra virgin olive oil

½ green cabbage, thinly sliced

½ cup sour cream

Juice of ½ lime

6 to 12 soft corn tortillas

2 cups cooked brown rice (page 192)

Prepare an outdoor grill or preheat broiler. Season the fish fillets with salt and pepper, then rub them with the olive oil. Place the fillets on the grill rack, or on a broiler pan and slip under the broiler. Grill or broil, turning once, until slightly browned on the outside, opaque but still moist inside, 5 to 7 minutes per side.

Cut the cooked fillets into slices about ¼ inch thick. (Keep your eye out for any bones you may have missed.) Cover and reserve.

In a medium mixing bowl, toss the cabbage with the sour cream and lime juice.

Heat the tortillas individually on a grill or dry skillet, or wrap 4 or 5 together in plastic wrap to warm in a microwave.

Place 2 or 3 slices of fish on a flat warmed tortilla. Top the fish with a dollop or two of mango salsa and then some cabbage. Wrap the ingredients with the tortilla. You should be able to pick up the taco in your hands, so try not to overload it.

Serve with the black bean salad and brown rice on the side.

Note: Canned coconut milk (traditionally obtained by shredding and pressing the meat of fresh coconut) is readily available in many grocery stores, often in the Hispanic or Asian foods section. It has a very subtle flavor.

CREAMY LOBSTER RISOTTO

There is perhaps no other seafood that can match the sweet, succulent character of lobster. This creamy, rich risotto is laced with buttery lobster chunks framed with a subtle, smoky tarragon edge.

Any lobster tails will do, but at PlumpJack, Maine lobster tails are preferred. They are smaller and sweeter than those taken from warmer waters. Be careful not to overcook the rice, or the risotto will become mushy or dried out. MAKES 4 MAIN COURSE SERVINGS OR 6 FIRST COURSE SERVINGS

AND IN YOUR GLASS

CHARDONNAY, SAUVIGNON BLANC, OR VIOGNIER ALL MAKE EXCELLENT WHITE-WINE PAIRING CHOICES HERE.

4 frozen Maine lobster tails (about 1½ pounds total weight), partially defrosted at room temperature for 1 to 2 hours

4 tablespoons (½ stick) unsalted butter

1 onion, finely chopped

2 cloves garlic, minced

1 cup Arborio rice

1½ cups homemade chicken stock (page 194) or canned low-sodium chicken broth

1 cup dry white wine

1 teaspoon dried tarragon

⅓ cup freshly grated Parmesan cheese

Coarse salt and freshly ground pepper

Place a steamer basket in a large pot and fill with water to reach just below the bottom of the basket. Place the lobster tails in the steamer, bring the water to a boil, reduce to simmer, and cover. Cook until the tails turn a light pink, 3 to 4 minutes. They should not be fully cooked or they will lose their firm texture later in the risotto. Remove the tails from the steamer and let them cool. Reserve about 2 cups of the steaming water.

When the lobster tails are cool enough to handle, use the point of a paring knife to score the underside of each tail, cutting lengthwise. Crack the tails open and pull out the meat. Chop it into small chunks, cover, and set aside.

In a large pot, heat 3 tablespoons of the butter over medium heat. Add the onion and garlic and cook until the onion is translucent, about 3 minutes. Add the rice and stir occasionally for 2 to 3 minutes. Add ½ cup of the chicken stock or broth, stirring frequently—but not constantly—until most of the liquid is absorbed, about 3 minutes. Continue adding the stock ½ cup at a time, stirring frequently until most is absorbed. When the stock has been incorporated, add the wine, stirring frequently until most is absorbed. Add the steaming water ½ cup at a time, stirring frequently until mostly absorbed. When the last of the lobster liquid is added, stir briefly and wait 2 minutes. Gently stir in the lobster chunks and the tarragon.

Keep the risotto simmering over medium-low heat and continue to stir at regular intervals. The risotto is ready to eat when the rice is tender but still slightly firm at the center of each grain, within 2 to 3 minutes. (The lobster will have finished cooking within a minute or so.) A creamy liquid should remain. Remove the risotto from the heat and stir in the cheese, the remaining 1 tablespoon butter, and salt and pepper to taste. Serve in broad, shallow bowls.

Panko-Crusted Calamari with Sweet and Tart Lemongrass/Chile Sauce

These fresh, crunchy calamari (otherwise known as squid) make a fabulous first course, but you can also enjoy them as a main course, perhaps on the heels of a green salad. Always use fresh squid, which is tender, as opposed to frozen squid, which can be rubbery. Cleaning squid is not much fun, but it's not difficult either. A much simpler solution is to ask your fishmonger to do it for you.

Note that the lemongrass/chile sauce is very intense—hot, tangy, and spicy.

MAKES 2 MAIN COURSE SERVINGS OR 4 FIRST COURSE SERVINGS

AND IN YOUR GLASS

PAIR THE CALAMARI WITH A CRISP SPARKLING WINE. A COLD BEER WOULD WORK WELL HERE, TOO.

FOR THE SAUCE

½ cup orange juice

¼ cup lime juice

2 tablespoons coarsely chopped lemongrass (see note on opposite page)

2 tablespoons coarsely chopped fresh ginger

1 clove garlic, coarsely chopped

⅓ cup Mae Ploy or any other commercial Thai sweet chile sauce (see note on opposite page)

In a blender or food processor, puree the orange juice, lime juice, lemongrass, ginger, and garlic. Pour the puree into a saucepan and add the Thai chile sauce. Bring to a boil, then reduce the heat and simmer for 15 minutes. Transfer to a small serving bowl and set aside.

FOR THE CALAMARI

Canola oil (about ½ to ⅔ quart)

2 cups panko (see note on page 101)

1½ cups all-purpose flour

½ cup cornstarch

1 teaspoon togarashi (a Japanese spice; see note on opposite page) or red pepper flakes

2 teaspoons coarse salt

1 pound fresh squid, cleaned, with tubes sliced in ½- to 1-inch-wide rounds, tentacles left whole

4 scallions, white and green parts, thinly sliced

2 or 3 lemons

In a large, deep, heavy sauté pan or skillet, pour the canola oil to a depth of 1 inch and heat over medium-high heat until you begin to see tiny bubbles starting to rise (about 365°F). Meanwhile, in a large mixing bowl, stir together the panko, flour, cornstarch, togarashi, and salt.

When the oil is hot, dredge the squid rounds and tentacles in the panko mixture and place them in the hot oil, taking care not to overfill the pan. (The squid pieces should be totally immersed in oil.) Fry until they are golden brown, 2 to 3 minutes. Do not overcook, or the squid will be chewy and tough. Use a slotted spoon to remove the cooked squid from the oil. Drain on paper towels. Depending on the size of your pan, you should be able to fry all the squid in one or two batches. Lower the heat slightly if the oil begins to smoke or splatter.

Transfer the calamari to a serving plate lined with paper towels. Garnish with the scallions, drizzle with juice from the lemons, and serve immediately with the lemongrass/chile sauce on the side for dipping.

Notes: Lemongrass is a perennial tropical plant. If necessary, peel off the outer layer of skin, which might be bruised, before slicing it into thin rounds or chopping it. You will need only a portion of a single stalk for this recipe. Look for lemongrass in your grocer's produce section.

Mae Ploy and togarashi can be found in the Asian foods section of many supermarkets.

Tiger Prawn Pasta with Pancetta and St. André Cheese Sauce

Creamy St. André cheese makes a fine foundation for a pasta sauce in this colorful dish. The white sauce serves as an excellent backdrop for tiger prawns, with their distinctive orange stripes. English peas add a sweet touch and present a third dimension to the color scheme as well.

If you have time, make the sauce in advance and store it in the refrigerator for up to three days. If you can't locate tiger prawns, any medium-size shrimp will do.

MAKES 4 SERVINGS

FOR THE CHEESE SAUCE

2 tablespoons unsalted butter	2 tablespoons all-purpose flour
1 shallot, minced	1 cup whole milk
1 clove garlic, minced	¼ pound St. André cheese

AND IN YOUR GLASS

YOU'LL NEED A WINE WITH BRIGHT ACIDITY TO BEST APPRECIATE THIS DISH. TRY SAUVIGNON BLANC OR RIESLING.

In a saucepan, melt the butter over low heat. Add the shallot and garlic and cook until the garlic is golden, 3 to 4 minutes. Whisk in the flour to create a soft paste. Add the milk, increase the heat to medium, and bring to a simmer, stirring regularly to prevent scorching. Simmer until the sauce thickens, 5 to 10 minutes.

Remove and discard the rind from the cheese. Cut the cheese into small pieces and stir them into the sauce until they melt. Let the sauce cool and transfer to a bowl or plastic container. Cover and refrigerate until ready to use. (Makes about 1 cup.)

FOR THE TIGER PRAWNS

⅓ cup sun-dried tomatoes (not oil-packed)	1½ cups dry white wine
Coarse salt	1 shallot, minced
1 pound fettuccine or other dried pasta	2 cloves garlic, minced
¼ pound pancetta, diced	¼ teaspoon red pepper flakes
1 tablespoon extra virgin olive oil	1 cup fresh English peas (about 1 pound in the shell)
1 pound tiger prawns, shelled	Freshly ground pepper

Soak the sun-dried tomatoes in hot water for 20 minutes. When they have softened, chop them coarsely.

Bring a large pot of salted water to a boil. Add the pasta and cook until tender but still firm, about 10 minutes. Meanwhile, begin cooking the rest of the dish.

In a large skillet or saucepan, cook the pancetta over medium heat, stirring occasionally, until it is crisp, 5 to 10 minutes. Using a slotted spoon, remove the pancetta from the pan and reserve. Drain the fat from the pan and discard. Without rinsing the pan, place it back over medium heat, add the olive oil, and return the pancetta to the pan. Add the prawns and cook until they are opaque, with bright orange stripes, about 1 minute per side.

Pour the wine into the pan and stir to dissolve any bits of pancetta or shrimp that may have stuck to the pan's surface. Bring to a boil, then reduce the heat to simmer. Add the shallot, garlic, sun-dried tomatoes, red pepper flakes, and peas and cook until the peas are tender, about 5 minutes. Turn off the heat and stir in ½ cup of the cheese sauce.

Drain the pasta and add it to the pan. Toss until the noodles separate and are evenly coated with sauce. For a richer, creamier dish, stir in more sauce to taste. Season with salt and pepper.

Cow Hollow

A Neighborhood True to Its Past

San Francisco's modern-day history really began some 150 years ago with the California Gold Rush, which attracted pioneers from around the world who arrived in San Francisco and never left. Among them were Italians, Chinese, and Japanese immigrants whose culinary traditions set the tone for the city's eclectic and contemporary dining scene today. These early immigrants and succeeding generations created a charming urban center by the sea that evolved into a hub for forward-thinking Californians. During the last twenty-five years, another wave of newcomers has joined the old guard to refine the art of fine living with a West Coast flair.

In the early days, the city's hilly topography created natural physical boundaries that made it easy for neighborhoods with distinct personalities to evolve separately. The area known as Cow Hollow was once exactly what its name implies: pastureland for dairy farmers living on the outskirts of a young city.

But the water view from the neighboring Presidio hills soon attracted the wealthy, who built their sprawling Victorian houses within walking distance of Cow Hollow's main thoroughfare, Fillmore Street. By the turn of the nineteenth century, the local elite were hungry for restaurants in which to congregate. Balboa Cafe opened its doors in 1913 and quickly became a dining hub for the social set. The kitchen has been supplying the neighborhood with its own version of San Francisco comfort food since that time—under the PlumpJack banner since 1995.

The 1960s brought flower power and the hippies to San Francisco, and their presence and influence was felt throughout the city's many enclaves, including Cow Hollow. In 1965, a new West Coast sound was emanating from the Bay Area, and Marty Balin—leader of the rock group Jefferson Airplane—launched a music lounge called the Matrix directly across the street from Balboa Cafe. The lounge opened with the Airplane's first public performance. Subsequently, the Matrix presented other budding musicians and groups like the Grateful Dead, the Doors, Santana, Janis Joplin, and even Bruce Springsteen, who gave his first San Francisco performance there. Times have changed, but the lounge still serves up plenty of music, mostly by DJs and local live music groups. Now called MATRIXFILLMORE, it is owned by the PlumpJack Group, which (not surprisingly) has added an extensive wine list to its menu of unique cocktail offerings.

Today, Cow Hollow boasts an extraordinary number of cafes and small merchants whose shops are tucked neatly into Fillmore and the surrounding commercial streets. Most storefronts are located in single- or two-story buildings built of wood milled in a bygone era. Pedestrians strolling along the area's residential blocks are greeted by an equally strong sense of times past. Here, on streets that have housed generations of San Franciscans, well-maintained period homes preserve Cow Hollow's historical character framed in architectural tradition.

Sea Scallops with King Trumpet Mushrooms and Meyer Lemon Relish

The slightly crunchy, tangy lemon relish, served as a garnish in this dish, offers a fine contrast to the smooth scallops and mushrooms.

Look for large, sweet day boat or diver scallops. Their pure flavors marry well with the subtle, mildly earthy qualities of king trumpet mushrooms, a member of the "oyster" family of mushrooms. The availability of certain mushrooms changes with the seasons. If you can't find king trumpets, try to find other distinctive wild mushrooms, such as porcinis or golden-hued chanterelles. Any of these mushrooms will raise the bar for flavor and complexity. However, don't be discouraged if you can only obtain common white button mushrooms. They, too, will add their own distinctive character.

Meyer lemons are not as tart as conventional lemons. In fact, they are believed to be derived from a cross between a lemon and an orange. Alas, Meyers are not as available year-round as traditional lemons, which are equally suitable for this dish. Make the relish in advance for greatest ease in the kitchen. MAKES 4 SERVINGS

AND IN YOUR GLASS

YOU'LL NOTICE THAT WHITE WINE IS USED TO COOK THE SCALLOPS AND MUSHROOMS. WE SUGGEST YOU ENJOY THE REST OF THE BOTTLE WITH YOUR MEAL. TRY A DRY, CRISP SAUVIGNON BLANC, PINOT BLANC, PINOT GRIS, OR CHARDONNAY, FOR EXAMPLE.

FOR THE RELISH

2 medium Meyer lemons

1 tablespoon unsalted butter

1 rib celery, diced

½ carrot, peeled and diced

½ parsnip, peeled and diced

Preheat oven to 400°F.

Roast 1 of the lemons for 15 minutes. (Be careful not to roast it much longer, or it will burst.) Remove it from the oven and let it cool.

While the lemon is roasting, melt the butter in a saucepan over medium heat. Add the celery, carrot, and parsnip and cook, stirring occasionally, until moderately soft, 5 to 10 minutes.

Transfer the vegetables to a bowl and add the juice of both the raw and roasted lemon. Using a paring knife, remove half the skin from the roasted lemon, finely chop it, and mix it in with the relish. Reserve at room temperature for up to several hours or refrigerate overnight.

continued on page 116

FOR THE SCALLOPS AND MUSHROOMS

1 tablespoon unsalted butter

16 large sea scallops

¼ cup dry white wine

½ pound king trumpet mushrooms, rinsed and thinly sliced (see headnote)

2 cups hot cooked white rice (page 192)

In a large sauté pan or skillet, melt the butter over medium-high heat. Add the scallops and sear on each side, about 2 minutes per side. Remove the scallops from the pan and reserve on a plate.

Add the wine to the pan and stir to dissolve any brown bits from the bottom. Add the mushrooms and stir to coat evenly with the liquid in the pan. Reduce the heat to medium and cook, stirring occasionally, until soft, 5 to 10 minutes. Return the scallops to the pan with the mushrooms for 1 minute to warm them.

Divide the scallop and mushroom mixture evenly among 4 plates. Place a mound of white rice and a small amount of the lemon relish next to the scallops.

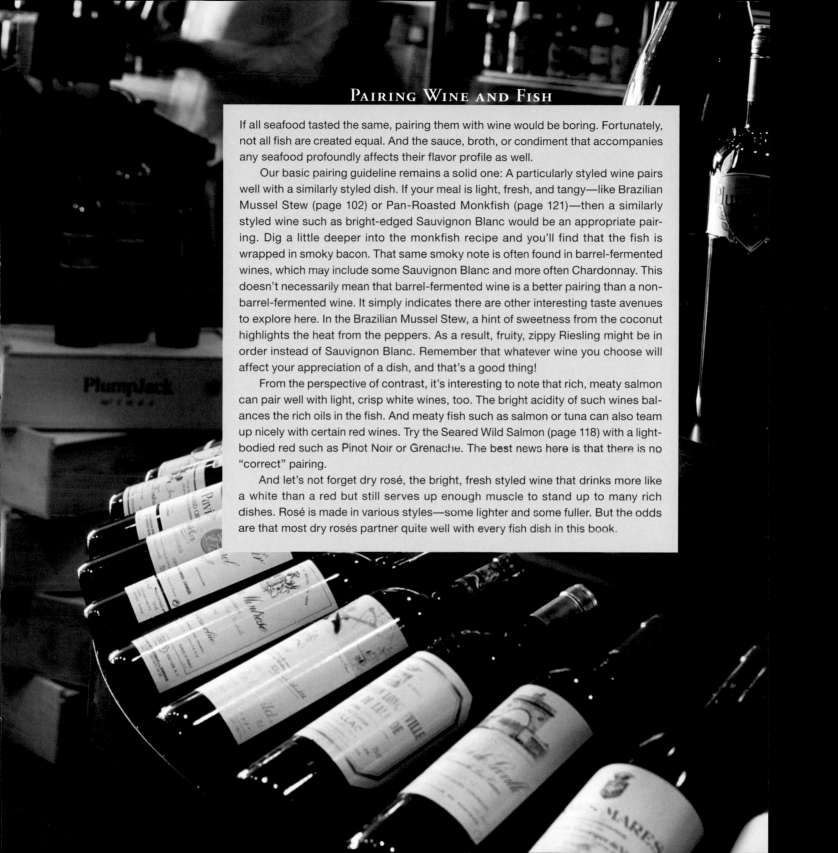

If all seafood tasted the same, pairing them with wine would be boring. Fortunately, not all fish are created equal. And the sauce, broth, or condiment that accompanies any seafood profoundly affects their flavor profile as well.

Our basic pairing guideline remains a solid one: A particularly styled wine pairs well with a similarly styled dish. If your meal is light, fresh, and tangy—like Brazilian Mussel Stew (page 102) or Pan-Roasted Monkfish (page 121)—then a similarly styled wine such as bright-edged Sauvignon Blanc would be an appropriate pairing. Dig a little deeper into the monkfish recipe and you'll find that the fish is wrapped in smoky bacon. That same smoky note is often found in barrel-fermented wines, which may include some Sauvignon Blanc and more often Chardonnay. This doesn't necessarily mean that barrel-fermented wine is a better pairing than a non-barrel-fermented wine. It simply indicates there are other interesting taste avenues to explore here. In the Brazilian Mussel Stew, a hint of sweetness from the coconut highlights the heat from the peppers. As a result, fruity, zippy Riesling might be in order instead of Sauvignon Blanc. Remember that whatever wine you choose will affect your appreciation of a dish, and that's a good thing!

From the perspective of contrast, it's interesting to note that rich, meaty salmon can pair well with light, crisp white wines, too. The bright acidity of such wines balances the rich oils in the fish. And meaty fish such as salmon or tuna can also team up nicely with certain red wines. Try the Seared Wild Salmon (page 118) with a light-bodied red such as Pinot Noir or Grenache. The best news here is that there is no "correct" pairing.

And let's not forget dry rosé, the bright, fresh styled wine that drinks more like a white than a red but still serves up enough muscle to stand up to many rich dishes. Rosé is made in various styles—some lighter and some fuller. But the odds are that most dry rosés partner quite well with every fish dish in this book.

Seared Wild Salmon on Fresh White Corn and Vegetable Sauté with Lemon/Tarragon Butter

This artful presentation offers a bright backdrop to frame the copper-hued salmon. Tarragon provides a bridge, subtly flavoring both the vegetables and the garnish. Try Skins-On Mashed Potatoes (page 92) as an accompaniment.

The Pacific Ocean is home to a long-celebrated population of wild salmon, which find their way back up the creeks and rivers of the West Coast each year to spawn. Wild salmon has less fat and is more delicately flavored than farm-raised salmon. But finding true wild salmon in the marketplace can be difficult. Fortunately, either wild or farm-raised fish will fit easily into this recipe. MAKES 4 SERVINGS

AND IN YOUR GLASS

LIGHTER RED WINES SUCH AS PINOT NOIR OR GRENACHE ARE RECOMMENDED. BY CONTRAST, ALMOST ANY WHITE WINE OR ROSÉ WITH CRISP ACIDITY WILL ALSO ENHANCE WHAT'S ON YOUR PLATE.

FOR THE BUTTER

2 tablespoons minced fresh tarragon

Zest of ½ lemon, coarsely chopped

4 tablespoons (½ stick) unsalted butter, softened

Using a fork, thoroughly mix the tarragon and the lemon zest into the butter. Refrigerate until ready to use.

FOR THE SALMON

3 tablespoons extra virgin olive oil

4 salmon fillets (about 6 ounces each)

Coarse salt and freshly ground pepper

Preheat oven to 400°F.

In a large ovenproof skillet or sauté pan, heat the oil over high heat until it shimmers. Season the salmon with salt and pepper on both sides and place the fillets in the pan, skin side up. Cook until a golden crust begins to appear on the bottoms of the fillets, 4 to 5 minutes. Place the pan in the oven. (Do not turn the fish over.) Bake until the fish is cooked medium, 6 to 7 more minutes. Remove the pan from the oven, flip the fish over onto its skin, and let rest for several minutes before serving.

continued on page 120

FOR THE VEGETABLES

2 tablespoons extra virgin olive oil

3 cups fresh white corn kernels (from 4 or 5 ears)

1 cup fresh shiitake mushrooms, stemmed and sliced

1 cup broccolini (baby broccoli) florets

2 tablespoons minced fresh tarragon

2 tablespoons minced fresh parsley

2 tablespoons unsalted butter

2 cups cherry tomatoes, halved

Coarse salt and freshly ground pepper

While the fish is in the oven, heat the olive oil in a medium pan over medium-high heat. Add the corn and sauté for 1 minute. Add the mushrooms and broccolini and sauté for 2 minutes, stirring often. Add the tarragon, parsley, and butter. Stir to mix well and sauté for 2 more minutes. Gently stir in the tomatoes and sauté for 30 seconds. Remove from the heat and season with salt and pepper.

Divide the vegetables among 4 dinner plates. Place a salmon fillet next to the vegetables. Garnish each fillet with a dollop of tarragon butter and, if using, a small mound of mashed potatoes on the side.

Pan-Roasted Monkfish with Basmati Rice and Coriander Broth

In this delicate yet satisfying dish, an intriguing, light-bodied broth frames meaty monkfish wrapped in smoky, salty bacon—perfect for a cold winter night spent with good friends.

Basmati rice originated in India, where the Hindi word *basmati* means "fragrant." It is light in color and long-grained, with a slightly nutty aroma. You can substitute any similar rice with good results. MAKES 4 SERVINGS

AND IN YOUR GLASS

ENJOY THIS DISH WITH A BOTTLE OF ANY CRISP, LIGHT-BODIED WHITE WINE, SUCH AS SAUVIGNON BLANC OR PINOT BLANC.

FOR THE BROTH

2 tablespoons extra virgin olive oil	5 sprigs cilantro, coarsely chopped
1 rib celery, finely chopped	2 teaspoons ground coriander
1 carrot, peeled and diced	4 cups fish stock (page 193)
½ onion, diced	1 teaspoon coarse salt

In a medium saucepan, heat the olive oil over medium heat until it shimmers. Stir in the celery, carrot, onion, cilantro, and coriander and cook for 2 minutes. Add the stock and the salt and bring to a boil, then reduce the heat and simmer for 15 minutes. Remove from the heat and cover to keep warm.

FOR THE RICE

1 tablespoon extra virgin olive oil	2 cups water
1 cup basmati rice	1 tablespoon unsalted butter

While the broth is simmering, heat the olive oil in a medium saucepan over medium heat until it shimmers. Add the rice and stir to coat the grains with the oil. Cook for 2 minutes, stirring occasionally. Add the water and butter and bring to a boil, then reduce to simmer, cover, and cook until all the liquid has been absorbed, 10 to 12 minutes. Set aside.

continued on page 123

FOR THE MONKFISH

2 monkfish tails (about 1½ pounds total weight)

4 slices bacon

2 tablespoons extra virgin olive oil

Coarse salt and freshly ground pepper

While the broth and rice are both simmering, preheat oven to 350°F. Wrap 2 slices of bacon around each fish tail so that it is entirely encased in bacon.

In a large ovenproof skillet or pan, heat the olive oil over medium-high heat until it shimmers. Lay both tails in the pan and cook for 3 minutes. Use a spatula and a wooden spoon to gently flip the tails, making sure they stay wrapped in the bacon, and cook for another 3 minutes. Place the pan in the oven and roast until the bacon has a finished look (although it will not be crisp) and the monkfish is opaque throughout, about 15 minutes.

Quickly reheat the broth over high heat. Place a mound of rice (about ½ cup) in each of 4 wide soup bowls. Cut the fish tails in half, leaving each half wrapped in 1 piece of bacon, and place each portion on top of a mound of rice. Evenly divide the broth among the 4 servings, pouring it over the fish and letting it settle into the rice. Season with salt and freshly ground pepper to taste.

Grilled Halibut with Orange/Fennel Puree, Asparagus, and Warm Quinoa Salad

This recipe takes simple meaty halibut steaks and elevates them to the centerpiece of an elegant, subtly complex, yet fully satisfying meal. Licorice-like fennel and citrus add an exotic edge, while the quinoa salad—made with those tiny couscous-like native American grains— offers a lightweight foil filled with flavor.

Note that blood oranges are seasonal. You can substitute any orange, but you'll lose the reddish hue in the puree. MAKES 4 SERVINGS

AND IN YOUR GLASS

CRISP, HERBAL, CITRUS-LIKE SAUVIGNON BLANC IS YOUR BEST BET FOR A WINE ACCOMPANIMENT.

FOR THE QUINOA SALAD

1½ cups vegetable stock (page 195) or canned low-sodium vegetable broth

½ cup white wine

1 cup quinoa

1 tablespoon plus ¼ cup extra virgin olive oil

1 carrot, peeled and diced

1 turnip, peeled and diced

Juice of 1 tangerine

Leaves from 3 sprigs tarragon, chopped

1 small bunch chives, minced

In a saucepan, bring the vegetable stock and wine to a boil over high heat. Stir in the quinoa and return to a boil, then cover, reduce the heat to low, and cook until all the liquid has been absorbed, 10 to 15 minutes. Remove from the heat and set aside, covered.

In another saucepan over medium-high heat, heat the 1 tablespoon olive oil until it shimmers. Sauté the carrot and turnip, stirring occasionally, until tender, about 10 minutes.

In a large bowl, gently and thoroughly mix the quinoa, the carrot/turnip mixture, the ¼ cup olive oil, and the tangerine juice, tarragon, and chives. Cover and set aside.

FOR THE ORANGE/FENNEL PUREE

½ fennel bulb, coarsely chopped

1 cup dry white wine

Juice of 1 blood orange

Place the fennel in a small saucepan and cover with the wine. If necessary, add water to cover the fennel completely with liquid. Bring to a boil, then reduce to simmer, uncovered, until the fennel is tender, 10 to 15 minutes. Combine the fennel and its remaining liquid with the blood orange juice in a blender or food processor. Pulse to make a coarse puree and reserve.

FOR SERVING

1½ pounds asparagus, tough ends trimmed

2 tablespoons olive oil

Coarse salt and freshly ground pepper

4 halibut steaks (about 6 ounces each)

In a large pan or skillet, boil enough water to cover the asparagus. Add the asparagus and cook for 2 minutes (it will be only partially cooked). Drain and rinse the asparagus in cold water to retain the color. Place the asparagus in a bowl and toss with 1 tablespoon of the olive oil and salt and pepper to taste. Set aside.

Prepare a hot grill or preheat oven broiler. Season the halibut steaks with salt and pepper and rub them evenly with the remaining 1 tablespoon olive oil. Cook the steaks on the grill or in a lightly oiled pan under the broiler until the flesh is white and flaky, 5 to 7 minutes per side. When the fish is nearly done, grill or broil the asparagus until tender, 3 to 4 minutes, turning occasionally.

Serve the halibut, flanked by asparagus and warm quinoa salad, on dinner plates. Top the halibut with a dollop of the fennel puree. Season with additional salt and pepper to taste.

POULTRY AND MEATS

While great meals certainly don't require protein, meat and fowl do satisfy a certain primal desire among many of us. With just a little salt and pepper, grilled meats—preferably medium-rare—celebrate the essence of our carnivorous heritage. The use of herbs, marinades, and sauces reveals complementary flavors and textures. And a well-chosen bottle of wine, blessed with natural acidity and the gentle grip of ripe tannins, can add just the right finishing touch (see "What Wine Should We Most Enjoy with Dinner?" on page 18).

Throughout this chapter, chicken, goose, rabbit, pork, beef, lamb, and venison are featured in dishes ranging from salads to sumptuous stews. Some of the recipes, such as Pork Carnitas Quesadillas (page 138), reflect California's deep-rooted Hispanic culture. Others, such as Thai Beef Salad (page 155) and Venison Ragout with Potato Gnocchi (page 163), show off the influence of later immigrants. The Balboa Burger (page 152) is renowned by burger aficionados in San Francisco, where it is a longtime signature dish at PlumpJack's Balboa Cafe. This classic burger, framed in a French baguette, offers a profoundly simple and pleasurable dining experience for any palate. At the other end of the culinary spectrum, dishes such as Twice-Cooked Pork Belly with Pear Salsa and Braised Endives (page 144) and Rabbit Pappardelle with Chanterelles (page 128) offer more complexity. In between, you will find dishes that are sure to satisfy a wide variety of tastes.

Rabbit Pappardelle with Chanterelles

Not so long ago, wild jackrabbits were fair game for vintners throughout Napa Valley. These long-eared critters feasted on the tender shoots of young grapevines and caused enough damage to earn a regular spot in the family stew pot. Today, farm-bred rabbits are much easier to come by at the local grocer. This recipe calls for only the rear and front legs because the meat serves basically as a condiment for the wide Italian egg noodles known as pappardelle. Ask your butcher for just the legs, or you'll have far more meat than required. Chanterelle mushrooms add buttery elegance, but they are not always in season. Any other mushroom will suffice if necessary.

A little forethought is required here, as the rabbit must cook in the oven for about an hour. The rest of the preparation is straightforward and fairly quick. MAKES 4 SERVINGS

AND IN YOUR GLASS

ENJOY THIS DISH WITH ANY POWERFUL RED WINE SUCH AS SYRAH OR CABERNET SAUVIGNON. OR TAKE A DIFFERENT TACK AND PAIR IT WITH AN EQUALLY ASSERTIVE WHITE WINE SUCH AS BARREL-FERMENTED CHARDONNAY OR GEWÜRZTRAMINER.

3 tablespoons extra virgin olive oil	10 sprigs thyme
Front and rear legs from 2 rabbits	5 sprigs sage
Coarse salt and freshly ground pepper	3 slices bacon, chopped
1 onion, diced	1 clove garlic, minced
2 carrots, 1 coarsely chopped, 1 thinly sliced	½ pound chanterelle mushrooms
2 parsnips, 1 coarsely chopped, 1 thinly sliced	½ pound cremini (or button) mushrooms
2 cups dry sherry	½ pound dried pappardelle noodles
2 bay leaves	2 tablespoons unsalted butter
1 teaspoon black peppercorns	2 tablespoons all-purpose flour

Preheat oven to 325°F.

In a Dutch oven or large, deep ovenproof pot, heat 1 tablespoon of the olive oil over high heat until it shimmers. Season the rabbit legs with salt and pepper and sear on both sides, about 30 seconds per side. Remove the legs from the pot and reserve.

Lower the heat to medium and add another tablespoon of olive oil. Add the onion and cook until translucent, about 3 minutes. Add the coarsely chopped carrot and parsnip and cook, stirring occasionally, until moderately soft, 5 to 10 minutes. Return the rabbit legs to the pot and add the sherry, bay leaves, peppercorns, thyme, sage, and enough water to cover the rabbit legs. Cover the pot and braise in the oven until the meat falls easily off the bone, about 1 hour.

Remove the legs from the pot, and when they have cooled enough to handle, pull the meat from the bones. Reserve the meat; discard the bones. Strain the liquid from the pot, reserve, and discard any remaining solids.

In a large skillet or saucepan, heat the remaining 1 tablespoon olive oil over medium heat until it moves easily in the pan. Add the bacon and cook until it begins to brown, about 5 minutes. Stir in the garlic and cook for another minute. Add the mushrooms and stir to coat with the oil. Cook, stirring occasionally, until slightly wilted, 3 to 5 minutes. Add the sliced carrot and parsnip and cook for 5 more minutes. Add the rabbit meat and 3 cups of the reserved rabbit broth. (You can freeze any extra broth and use it as you would a chicken stock for another occasion.) Bring the broth to a boil, reduce the heat to medium, and simmer for 5 more minutes.

Meanwhile, cook the pappardelle noodles in boiling water (lightly salted, if desired) until tender but still firm, about 7 minutes. Drain in a colander and shake dry.

In a small saucepan, slowly melt the butter over medium-low heat and gently whisk in the flour. Stir until the mixture browns, about 1 minute. Whisk this roux into the rabbit broth and simmer, stirring, until the sauce thickens. Add the noodles and toss, coating them thoroughly with the rabbit sauce. Garnish individual servings with coarse salt and freshly ground pepper to taste.

Southern Fried Chicken Breasts with Wild Mushroom Gravy and Red Vegetable Hash

Inspired by the traditional cuisine of America's South, this recipe features plump chicken breasts coated with a delightfully crunchy, golden brown batter. The accompanying red-hued vegetable hash serves up an earthy, herbal supplement. A creamy mushroom gravy dresses the chicken handsomely.

It's worth looking for "hen-of-the-woods" mushrooms, or *maitake,* as they are called in Japan, for a truly excellent gravy. This distinctive wild variety, with its feather-like headdress, has long been appreciated by the Asian community not only for its delicate forest and mineral flavors, but also for its medicinal properties, which are said to enhance the immune system. However, any mushroom or blend of mushrooms—from buttery chanterelles to cultivated creminis and portobellos—will make a fine gravy.

The chicken breasts need to marinate for several hours prior to cooking. But it's best to cook the vegetable hash and the mushroom gravy about an hour before you start frying the chicken. Then, once the chicken breasts are ready to eat, the hash and gravy can be quickly reheated on the stovetop for easy serving. MAKES 6 SERVINGS

AND IN YOUR GLASS

CHICKEN TEAMS UP EASILY WITH ALMOST ANY KIND OF WINE. HERE, WITH MUSHROOMS AND BEETS AT THE FORE, TRY PINOT NOIR OR SYRAH. BOTH VARIETALS ARE BLESSED WITH ATTRACTIVE EARTH TONES THAT ECHO THE NATURAL CHARACTERISTICS OF THE MUSHROOMS AND ROOT VEGETABLES. WHITE-WINE LOVERS SHOULD TRY A LUSH, OAK-AGED CHARDONNAY, VIOGNIER, OR CHENIN BLANC. A LIGHTWEIGHT WHITE WILL BE LOST IN THE CREAMY RICHNESS OF THIS DISH.

FOR THE MARINADE

2 cups buttermilk

½ teaspoon cayenne pepper

1 tablespoon coarse salt

1 tablespoon minced fresh rosemary

2 teaspoons freshly ground black pepper

6 boneless, skinless chicken breasts (8 ounces each)

In a large bowl, mix the buttermilk and cayenne. In a small bowl, combine the salt, rosemary, and pepper. Sprinkle the salt mixture onto both sides of the chicken breasts. (Discard any excess salt mix.) Immerse the chicken breasts in the buttermilk marinade and refrigerate for 2 hours.

continued on page 132

FOR THE HASH

2 beets, trimmed, peeled, and halved	1 cup peeled, diced sweet potato
8 tablespoons (1 stick) unsalted butter	1 cup diced fennel bulb
1 cup diced onion	2 teaspoons minced fresh rosemary
2 cups peeled, diced russet potato	¼ teaspoon freshly grated nutmeg
1 cup diced carrot	1 cup heavy cream
1 cup diced parsnip	Coarse salt and freshly ground pepper

In a steamer, steam the beets until they are tender, 10 to 15 minutes. When the beets are cool enough to handle, grate them on the big holes of a box grater and set aside.

While the beets are cooking, in a large skillet or sauté pan, melt the butter over medium heat. Add the onion and cook until translucent, 2 to 3 minutes. Increase the heat to medium-high and add the potato, carrot, parsnip, sweet potato, and fennel. Mix well and sauté until the vegetables are lightly browned and tender, 10 to 15 minutes. Stir in the rosemary, nutmeg, and grated beets, then stir in the cream. Reduce the heat to medium-low and simmer, stirring occasionally, until the cream is absorbed, about 15 minutes. Season with salt and pepper to taste, remove from the heat, cover, and set aside.

FOR THE GRAVY

8 tablespoons (1 stick) unsalted butter	½ cup dry sherry
2 tablespoons minced onion	1 cup heavy cream
1 tablespoon minced fresh rosemary	½ teaspoon coarse salt
1 pound wild or cultivated mushrooms, sliced or coarsely chopped	Freshly ground pepper

In a large skillet or sauté pan, melt the butter over medium heat. Add the onion and rosemary and cook until the onion is translucent, 2 to 3 minutes. Add the mushrooms and stir to coat with the butter. Cook until slightly wilted, about 5 minutes. Add the sherry and stir to dissolve any browned bits that may be sticking to the bottom of the pan. Simmer for 1 minute. Add the cream, increase the heat to medium-high, and bring to a boil. Reduce the heat and simmer until the liquid is reduced by one-third, about 10 minutes. Season with the salt and pepper to taste. Remove the pan from the heat, cover, and set aside.

FOR THE CHICKEN

1¾ to 2 quarts canola oil	1 teaspoon freshly ground black pepper
4 cups all-purpose flour	
1 tablespoon coarse salt	½ teaspoon cayenne pepper

Pour the oil into a large, heavy, deep (5 to 6 inches deep) pot, filling it no more than two-thirds full. Heat the oil over medium-high heat to 375°F. It should begin to glisten and shimmer but should not smoke.

Meanwhile, in a large bowl, stir together the flour, salt, black pepper, and cayenne. Remove the chicken breasts from the marinade but reserve the marinade. Dredge each breast in the seasoned flour, then dip it back in the marinade. Dredge one more time in the flour.

Carefully place the chicken in the hot oil. (You may not have enough room to cook all 6 breasts at once, so try frying them in two batches.) Fry the breasts until they are golden brown, about 15 minutes, turning them from time to time, and transfer them to a plate lined with paper towels. (If desired, keep the chicken warm in a preheated 200°F oven. This fried chicken is also delicious at room temperature.)

Reheat the vegetable hash and the mushroom gravy separately over medium-high heat, stirring to warm evenly. Place a fried chicken breast on each plate, with a serving of the hash next to it. Garnish each breast with the gravy.

COOKING WITH WINE

Wine plays an important role as an ingredient for a number of recipes in this book. In some, wine's natural acidity acts as a tenderizer. In others, that same acidity serves to highlight flavor.

Should a recipe require only a small amount of wine, then by all means use a bit of what you plan to serve alongside your meal. But if, for example, 4 cups are required, you needn't use an expensive, high-end wine. The very qualities that make such a wine valuable will be boiled or cooked away on the stovetop or in the oven. In these instances, remember to purchase two different wines—one for the pot and one for the table.

Ironically, the only wines that should never be used in cooking are those labeled "cooking wine" in the supermarket. Typically, they are salted or otherwise adulterated to prevent children from purchasing and drinking them. With their added ingredients, these wines will not only throw off recipe measurements but also add their bizarre flavors to the sauce.

Rosemary Roast Chicken with New Potatoes and Carrots

Roast chicken remains a centerpiece comfort food for so many of us. In this version, fresh rosemary is the key ingredient, adding its distinctive herbal stamp to all components of the dish. As the chicken cooks, its rosemary-scented aromas will fill your kitchen and set the stage for a mouthwatering dinner. Fruity extra virgin olive oil adds a measure of sweetness while sealing in the flavors of the bird. The potatoes, carrots, and garlic cloves roasting in the chicken pan become infused with heady flavors of herb and oil, evoking the rustic elegance of simple country cooking. Lovers of garlic can suck the cooked garlic directly from the roasted cloves.

Use leftover chicken to make Curried Chicken and Spinach Salad (page 65) and save the carcass for chicken stock (page 194). MAKES 4 SERVINGS

AND IN YOUR GLASS

CHICKEN WILL EASILY PAIR UP WITH MANY RED OR WHITE WINES. WITH THIS DISH, TRY A FRUIT-FORWARD ZINFANDEL OR PINOT NOIR AMONG REDS. EARTHY SYRAH WOULD ALSO MAKE A FINE RED-WINE CHOICE. SIMILARLY, AMONG WHITE WINES, A FRUITY VIOGNIER, RIESLING, OR CHARDONNAY WOULD SERVE WELL.

1 chicken (3 to 4 pounds), rinsed and patted dry

Coarse salt and freshly ground pepper

3 tablespoons extra virgin olive oil

3 tablespoons coarsely chopped fresh rosemary

2 pounds red-skinned or white potatoes, scrubbed and cut into 2-inch chunks

4 carrots, peeled and cut into 1- to 2-inch lengths

8 cloves garlic, unpeeled

Preheat oven to 400°F.

Lightly season the outside of the chicken with salt and pepper. Gently rub the skin with 1 tablespoon of the olive oil and 2 tablespoons of the rosemary. Set the chicken, breast side up, on a rack in a roasting pan.

In a large bowl, toss the potatoes, carrots, and garlic cloves with the remaining 2 tablespoons olive oil and 1 tablespoon rosemary. Add salt and pepper to taste and toss again.

Place the vegetables in the roasting pan around the rack and under the chicken. Set the pan in the oven and roast until the chicken skin is crisp and the juices run clear when a thigh is pierced, 1 hour 10 minutes to 1½ hours. (The temperature of the inner thigh should be 180°F.)

Transfer the chicken to a cutting board and let rest for 5 minutes prior to carving. Place the vegetables in a serving bowl; they can be served alongside the sliced chicken. Use the drippings from the bottom of the pan to drizzle over the carved meat.

Goose Breast with Red Wine Gravy and Wild Rice with Mushrooms and Toasted Pine Nuts

Goose, like duck, has a seductive, earthy quality. Here, it shares the spotlight with an almost-crunchy and complex wild rice and would pair beautifully with a winter vegetable like Braised Red Cabbage with Bacon (page 90). Typically, you won't find goose breasts sitting on the shelf at your supermarket with the chicken breasts. Ask your butcher to order them from one of the many specialty meats purveyors now operating throughout the nation.

These meaty goose breasts are simple to prepare. For greatest ease in the kitchen, make the rice—and any other side dishes you might like to serve as well—in advance. Other side dishes can also be kept warm or be reheated, which will leave you free to cook the breasts to order with minimum fuss.

Even if you prefer your meats well-done, try eating goose medium-rare. When overcooked, it becomes tough and flavorless. And remember, you don't need to wait for Christmas to eat goose! MAKES 4 OR 5 SERVINGS

AND IN YOUR GLASS

ENJOY THIS DISH WITH A FULL-BODIED RED WINE SUCH AS CABERNET SAUVIGNON, MERLOT, OR SYRAH.

1 tablespoon unsalted butter

2 tablespoons all-purpose flour

2 cups chicken stock (page 194) or canned low-sodium chicken broth

1 cup dry red wine

Coarse salt and freshly ground pepper

2 full boneless goose breasts (about 1½ pounds each), split

Wild Rice with Mushrooms and Toasted Pine Nuts (page 97)

Preheat oven to 400°F.

In a medium saucepan, melt the butter over medium heat. Stir or whisk in the flour to form a paste and cook, stirring often, until it becomes nut brown, about 3 minutes. Add the stock and whisk to mix. Bring to a boil, whisking constantly. Reduce the heat and simmer, whisking occasionally, until the gravy has reduced by half, about 15 minutes.

In a small saucepan, bring the wine to a boil. Reduce the heat to medium and simmer until the wine is reduced by half. When both the wine and the chicken stock are reduced, stir the wine into the stock, add salt and pepper to taste, cover, and reserve until ready to use. Reheat the gravy immediately before serving.

Using a fork, poke 4 or 5 sets of holes in the skin of each goose breast. Season both sides of the breasts with salt and pepper.

Heat a large ovenproof pan or skillet over medium-high heat. When the pan is hot, add the breasts skin side down and cook until the skin is browned and crisp, 7 to 8 minutes. Remove the breasts from the pan and discard the fat that has accumulated in the bottom. Place the breasts back in the pan—this time skin side up—put the pan in the oven, and roast until they are medium-rare, 8 to 10 minutes.

Slice each breast into $\frac{1}{4}$-inch-thick strips (no need to let them rest), drizzle with hot gravy, and serve at once with the rice and, if using, any other winter vegetables.

Pork Carnitas Quesadillas with Guacamole and Tomato Salsa

This pan-fried tortilla—filled with succulent, slow-cooked pork and topped with a salsa designed to warm cold bodies—is a hungry skier's delight. Don't write it off for warm weather, though. Quesadillas are for year-round enjoyment.

Make this dish in stages. The components are all easy to prepare, but organization is key. The carnitas, or shredded pork, requires more than two hours in the oven, so start by planning ahead. (The fragrant aromas of braising pork are guaranteed to inspire the palate.) The caramelized onions take more than an hour in the pan, so start them about an hour after the pork has begun to cook. The salsa also needs to simmer on the stovetop and then settles at room temperature for a half hour. Guacamole is quick, though, and can be made shortly before the quesadillas are prepared for pan-frying. MAKES 12 TO 15 QUESADILLAS, OR 4 TO 6 SERVINGS

AND IN YOUR GLASS

MEXICAN FOOD WORKS WELL WITH BEER, BUT IT'S EQUALLY GOOD—IF NOT BETTER—WITH THE RIGHT KIND OF WINE. FOR THESE QUESADILLAS, A FRUITY, DRY GEWÜRZTRAMINER OR RIESLING WOULD SERVE WELL. DRY ROSÉ CAN ALSO FIND FAVOR HERE. RED-WINE LOVERS MIGHT FOCUS ON FRUIT-FORWARD, SOFT-TEXTURED VARIETALS SUCH AS PINOT NOIR, GRENACHE, AND ZINFANDEL.

FOR THE CARNITAS

2 pounds boneless pork butt	4 or 5 cloves garlic, peeled
4 cups chicken stock (page 194) or canned low-sodium chicken broth	1 teaspoon red pepper flakes
	1 bay leaf
1 cup fresh orange juice (from 3 to 4 oranges)	1 teaspoon fennel seeds
¼ cup maple syrup	1 teaspoon cumin seeds
1 ancho (or pasilla) chile, seeded and stemmed	1 cinnamon stick
	1 teaspoon coarse salt
1 onion, quartered	¼ teaspoon freshly ground pepper

Preheat oven to 375°F.

Place all the ingredients in a Dutch oven or large, deep ovenproof pot. Cover, place in the oven, and braise until the meat is tender, about 2 hours. Uncover the pot, turn the meat so that the moist underside is now facing up, and continue to cook, uncovered, for another half hour. Remove the meat from the pot and let cool for 15 minutes. Using your hands, shred the meat into small pieces and reserve.

Discard the liquid and other solids. (Or strain, defat, and refrigerate the liquid. Although the liquid is not part of this recipe, reheat it as a tangy sauce for any number of dishes from rice to grilled meats or fish.)

FOR THE ONIONS

3 tablespoons extra virgin olive oil   3 medium onions, sliced

In a saucepan or heavy skillet, heat the olive oil over medium heat until it moves easily in the pan. Add the onions and stir to coat evenly with the oil. Reduce the heat to low and cook for about 1 hour, stirring every 10 minutes, until the onions are soft and slightly browned. Add more oil if necessary to prevent burning. Reserve.

FOR THE SALSA

¼ cup extra virgin olive oil

½ onion, coarsely chopped

6 plum tomatoes, cut into quarters or eighths

1 jalapeño pepper, seeded, stemmed, and coarsely chopped

2 garlic cloves, peeled

Coarse salt

¼ teaspoon ground cumin

¼ teaspoon ground coriander

¼ teaspoon chile powder

5 sprigs cilantro, coarsely chopped

Juice of 2 limes

In a large, heavy skillet, heat the olive oil over medium-high heat until it shimmers. Add the onion, tomatoes, jalapeño, garlic, and ¼ teaspoon salt and cook, stirring occasionally, until the tomatoes have released their juices and thickened, 10 to 15 minutes. Pour the tomato mixture into a large bowl and stir in the cumin, coriander, chile powder, cilantro, and lime juice. Cover and let sit for 30 minutes. Place the salsa in a blender or food processor and pulse 4 to 6 times to make a coarse puree; don't overprocess. Add more salt to taste, transfer to a small serving bowl, cover, and reserve. (Makes about 2 cups.)

FOR THE GUACAMOLE

2 avocados, pitted and peeled

1 teaspoon fresh lemon juice

1 small clove garlic, minced

¼ teaspoon coarse salt

Freshly ground pepper

Using a fork, mash the avocados in a bowl until fairly smooth. Add the lemon juice, garlic, salt, and pepper to taste, and mix well. Cover and reserve. (Makes about 2 cups.)

 *continued on page 140*

FOR THE QUESADILLAS

3 cups grated Monterey Jack cheese

8 to 10 sprigs cilantro, chopped

2 tablespoons canola oil, plus more oil as needed

12 to 15 soft flour tortillas (about 10 inches in diameter)

2 or 3 limes, cut into wedges

4 cups cooked black beans, dried (page 200) or canned, heated (optional)

Place the cheese and cilantro in a large mixing bowl. Add the carnitas and caramelized onions and mix well. Spread ½ cup of the carnitas mixture onto each tortilla. Fold the tortillas in half.

In a large, heavy skillet, heat the 2 tablespoons canola oil over medium-high heat. Fry the filled tortillas until each side is slightly brown, about 3 minutes per side. Add more oil to the pan as needed. Cut each quesadilla in half and top each half with a dollop of guacamole and salsa. Garnish with the lime wedges. Serve with black beans on the side, if you'd like.

Add more oil to the skillet as necessary for additional quesadillas. Lower the heat to medium as the pan heats up or if it begins to smoke.

Pork Chops with Sweet Corn Maque Choux

Pork is a sweet meat that teams up beautifully with the Cajun-inspired creamed corn known as *maque choux*. Pan-fried and topped with crunchy fried garlic, it marries with the subtle heat from the cayenne in the corn. For a classic comfort-food combo, serve this dish with Sautéed Kale (page 86), also blessed with a touch of garlic, for continuity of flavor.

Start cooking the maque choux first. The pork and greens can be prepared as the corn simmers. MAKES 4 SERVINGS

AND IN YOUR GLASS

THIS DISH CRIES OUT FOR FRUITY, OFF-DRY RIESLING IN YOUR GLASS. SPICY GEWÜRZTRAMINER OR RICH, BARREL-FERMENTED CHARDONNAY COULD BE EQUALLY EFFECTIVE. RED-WINE DIEHARDS SHOULD SEEK OUT LIGHT-BODIED, FRUIT-FORWARD PINOT NOIR, GRENACHE, OR SANGIOVESE, FOR EXAMPLE.

FOR THE MAQUE CHOUX

2 tablespoons unsalted butter

½ cup diced onion

½ cup diced red bell pepper

3 cups fresh white corn kernels (from 4 or 5 ears)

⅛ teaspoon cayenne pepper

2 plum or small tomatoes, coarsely chopped

Coarse salt

½ cup heavy cream

Freshly ground black pepper

In a large skillet, melt the butter over medium heat. Add the onion and cook until translucent, about 3 minutes. Add the corn, bell pepper, and cayenne, and stir to blend well. Cook for 8 to 10 minutes, stirring occasionally to prevent burning. Add the tomatoes, season with salt, and cook for 10 more minutes, stirring occasionally. Stir in the cream and cook for 2 more minutes. Season with freshly ground black pepper to taste. Remove from the heat, cover to keep warm, and serve as soon as the pork chops are done.

continued on page 143

FOR THE PORK CHOPS

4 thick pork chops (6 to 8 ounces each)	8 to 10 large cloves garlic, thinly sliced
Coarse salt and freshly ground pepper	2 cups dry white wine
2 tablespoons extra virgin olive oil	2 tablespoons unsalted butter

Season the pork chops with salt and pepper. In a large sauté pan or skillet, heat the olive oil over medium heat and cook the garlic until it is golden brown. Use a slotted spoon to transfer the garlic to a small bowl and set aside. Increase the heat under the pan to medium-high.

Place the pork chops in the hot pan, cover, and cook for 10 to 15 minutes per side, until the exterior is golden brown. (If the pan starts to smoke, add a tablespoon or two of the wine.) Transfer the pork chops to a plate and cover loosely with aluminum foil.

Add the rest of the wine to the pan and stir to dissolve any solids that might be stuck to the bottom. Increase the heat to high and cook to reduce the liquid by half, 2 to 3 minutes. Reduce the heat to low and add the butter, stirring until it has melted. Turn off the heat.

Place a pork chop on each plate, flanked by a mound of the corn maque choux. Garnish each chop with plenty of garlic and drizzle with the pan sauce.

Twice-Cooked Pork Belly with Pear Salsa and Braised Endives

This is a dish full of wonderfully complex flavors, yet made with exquisitely simple ingredients. Pork belly (essentially a slab of bacon that has not been cured or sliced) is slow-cooked to perfect tenderness and garnished with an almost crunchy pear salsa. The pork fat, which is buttery rich, begs to be eaten with a forkful of pear and endive. (Just for the record, lard—or pig fat—has only half the saturated fat of palm oil or coconut oil. And it has about one-third less saturated fat than butter.)

The dish does require a bit of time and planning in the kitchen. The meat is slowly cooked for about two hours and then chilled for at least another hour before the endives and final pork preparations are made. This first cooking and subsequent refrigeration of the pork belly could actually be done a day in advance, if you have time constraints the day of your dinner party. The rest of the recipe is comparatively quickly done and can be easily executed on the day of the event. MAKES 4 SERVINGS

AND IN YOUR GLASS

WHITE WINE, SWEET OR DRY, IS PROBABLY YOUR BEST BET HERE. WHAT'S IMPORTANT IS THAT IT SHOULD CONTAIN A GOOD DOSE OF ACIDITY TO BALANCE THE LUSHNESS OF THE DISH. TRY A SWEET-EDGED RIESLING ON ONE OCCASION AND A MINERAL-LIKE SAUVIGNON BLANC ON ANOTHER. EACH WILL ENHANCE YOUR PALATE IN A DIFFERENT MANNER.

FOR THE SALSA

1 tablespoon honey

1 tablespoon apple cider vinegar

2 firm pears (such as Bosc)

In a mixing bowl, whisk together the honey and vinegar. Peel the pears and remove the cores. Slice the pears into thin strips and dice them. Add the pears to the mixing bowl, stir, cover, and refrigerate until ready to use.

FOR THE PORK BELLY

2 pounds boneless pork belly

1 tablespoon canola or other vegetable oil

2 ribs celery, diced

1 carrot, diced

1 medium onion, diced

1 bay leaf

1 teaspoon black peppercorns

1 teaspoon dried thyme

1 teaspoon coarse salt

4 cups chicken stock (page 194) or canned low-sodium chicken broth

Preheat oven to 300°F.

Cut the pork belly lengthwise into 2- to 3-inch-wide strips. (You will end up with 3 or 4 wide slabs of pork belly.) In a Dutch oven or large, deep ovenproof pot, heat the canola oil over medium-high heat until it shimmers. Add the pork belly slabs and brown them on all sides,

continued on page 146

1 to 2 minutes per side. Remove the pork and set aside. Reduce the heat to medium, add the celery and carrot, and cook, stirring occasionally, for 5 minutes. Add the onion and cook, stirring occasionally, until translucent, about 5 more minutes. Add the bay leaf, peppercorns, thyme, and salt and stir to mix.

Place the pork back in the pot and pour in the chicken stock. Bring the stock to a boil. Cover the pot and place it in the oven; braise until the meat is fall-apart tender, about 2 hours. Remove the pot from the oven, uncover, and let the pork cool to room temperature. Carefully remove the pork belly slabs from the liquid and place them on a plate. Cover the meat with another plate to press it down a bit. Refrigerate until cold and firm, at least 1 hour.

Strain and reserve the liquid remaining in the pot. Discard the solids. The fat in the liquid will quickly rise to the top. Use a shallow ladle or a spoon to carefully skim off most of the fat and discard. Cover and refrigerate the remaining liquid.

FOR THE ENDIVES

6 Belgian endives, halved lengthwise	1 tablespoon sugar
Coarse salt	½ cup dry white wine
1 tablespoon honey	

Season the endives lightly with salt. In a large skillet, stir the honey and sugar together over medium heat until golden brown, about 1 minute. Place each endive half in the pan, cut side down, increase the heat to medium-high, and cook for 1 minute. Add the wine and enough water to cover the endives. Bring to a boil, then reduce the heat and simmer, uncovered, until the endives are tender, 8 to 10 minutes. Cover to keep warm.

TO FINISH THE DISH

1 tablespoon honey	1 tablespoon extra virgin olive oil
1 tablespoon apple cider vinegar	Freshly ground pepper

When you are ready to serve, preheat oven to 350°F.

Remove the meat and the reserved cooking liquid from the refrigerator. Any remaining fat will have congealed at the top of the liquid. Remove it with a spoon and discard. In a small saucepan, bring the liquid to a boil over high heat. Stir in the honey and vinegar and reduce the heat to medium, simmering until it becomes a thick sauce, 7 to 10 minutes. Reserve and reheat over high heat immediately prior to serving.

While the sauce is simmering, cut the pork belly into ¼-inch slices. In a large ovenproof skillet, heat the olive oil over medium heat until it shimmers. Brown the pork until crisp on the outside, about 3 minutes per side. (Be careful not to let the slices fall apart when flipping them, and watch out for spattering hot oil.) Then place the skillet in the oven for 3 to 5 minutes to finish cooking. Remove the pan from the oven and use a spatula to carefully transfer the pork to a plate lined with paper towels.

Evenly divide the pork belly slices among 4 dinner plates, arranging them in the center of each plate. Place a large dollop or two of the pear salsa alongside the pork. Arrange the endives to frame the outer edge of each plate. Spoon the reheated sauce over the meat. Garnish with freshly ground pepper to taste.

MUSTARD AND MEYER LEMON PORK TENDERLOIN WITH DRY JACK POLENTA

Mustard and Meyer lemon create a subtly delicious blend of flavors that are supported admirably by tender, juicy pork loin. A touch of chile adds high notes, but not in excess.

Meyer lemon, a cross between a lemon and an orange, is mellower on the palate than lemon and displays a hint of the sweetness found in oranges and tangerines. This golden citrus fruit is believed to have been developed in China and was brought to the United States by Frank Meyer, an American agricultural specialist who found it growing near Beijing in the early 1900s. Look for Meyer lemons from fall to early spring. If you can't find them for this recipe, substitute regular lemons.

That quintessential San Francisco cheese—Dry Jack—adds a decidedly West Coast dimension to the polenta. Dry Jack is a hard cow's milk cheese that was created in San Francisco in the early 1900s. It is best when aged two to three years, after which time it takes on a nutty, fruity flavor. Those who can't find Dry Jack can substitute aged Gouda.

Hearty Sautéed Kale (page 86) is an excellent addition to the plate. To ensure that the three components of this dish are ready to eat at the same time, make sure that all ingredients for the polenta and kale are prepped and laid out in advance. This will facilitate preparation while the pork is simmering and settling. MAKES 4 TO 6 SERVINGS

AND IN YOUR GLASS

TRY DRINKING A FRUITY WHITE RIESLING, GEWÜRZTRAMINER, OR CHARDONNAY. THOSE LOOKING FOR A RED-WINE ACCOMPANIMENT MIGHT ENJOY A LIGHTER-STYLED VARIETAL SUCH AS PINOT NOIR, GRENACHE, OR SANGIOVESE.

FOR THE PORK TENDERLOIN

1 tablespoon Dijon mustard

1 teaspoon mustard seeds

1 tablespoon chopped Meyer lemon zest

1 teaspoon Meyer lemon juice

1 tablespoon honey

2 teaspoons grated fresh ginger

1 tablespoon minced scallion (white part only)

1 tablespoon seeded, minced jalapeño pepper

2 teaspoons coarse salt

¼ teaspoon cayenne pepper

Freshly ground black pepper

2 pork tenderloins (2 to 2½ pounds total weight)

3 tablespoons extra virgin olive oil

In a small bowl, combine the mustard, mustard seeds, lemon zest, lemon juice, honey, ginger, scallion, jalapeño, salt, cayenne, and black pepper. Mix well with a wooden spoon or small whisk, making a moist rub. Coat the pork loins with the rub, set them on a plate, and refrigerate, uncovered, for 1 hour.

Heat the olive oil in a large sauté pan or skillet over high heat until it shimmers. Sear the pork loins on all sides until browned, about 3 minutes. Lower the heat to medium, cover the pan, and cook until the centers of the loins are light pink, 12 to 15 minutes. Transfer to a large plate or cutting board, cover with aluminum foil, and let rest 5 to 7 minutes.

This is a good time to begin cooking the kale and polenta.

FOR THE POLENTA

2½ cups water	¼ cup grated Dry Jack cheese
2 cups heavy cream	¼ cup freshly grated Parmesan cheese
2 tablespoons unsalted butter	1 teaspoon coarse salt
1 cup polenta	Freshly ground pepper

In a medium saucepan, combine the water, cream, and butter. Bring to a boil and slowly stir in the polenta with a whisk or wooden spoon. Reduce the heat to low and cook, stirring frequently with a wooden spoon, until creamy, 8 to 10 minutes (you should still be able to feel the texture of the grain in your mouth). Remove from the heat and stir in the cheeses and salt. Add freshly ground pepper to taste and set aside until ready to use. The polenta will become more solid the longer it sits.

Slice the pork into 1-inch-thick medallions. Serve each portion of pork flanked by some polenta and kale, if using, and spoon on any juices from the pork.

SQUAW VALLEY

THE MOUNTAINS

Perhaps it's the altitude, but all who visit Squaw Valley experience a rush of adrenaline and jaw-dropping awe. This panoramic collection of peaks, cliffs, and valleys is set high in the Sierra Nevada, about a four-hour drive north of San Francisco. In summer, majestic forests hug the steep slopes like an evergreen carpet. When the weather turns cold, a deep snow blanket covers the land, turning the lush green of summer to a stark white, punctuated now and then by blue-green crystalline waterfalls, frozen until spring. Given its formidable natural attributes, it's no wonder Squaw Valley—at 6,000 feet above sea level—beat out the pride of Europe's ski slopes to become the site of the 1960 Olympic Winter Games. Today, the valley's 34 lifts can carry 49,000 skiers per hour to varying levels of its vertiginous terrain.

Long before the 1960 Olympics, these mountains were magnets for European ski pioneers searching for challenges similar to those they had previously known in the Alps. But it was a native of nearby Reno, Nevada, Wayne Poulsen—skier, World War II pilot, and general visionary—who first saw Squaw Valley's potential to become a top-flight ski resort. In 1948, he brought in investor Alex Cushing to help create the Squaw Valley Development Corporation. Their partnership was ill-fated and dissolved several years later, but not before a seed had been planted.

It began in 1949, on Thanksgiving, with a small lodge, a rope tow, and a single ski lift billed as the longest double chairlift in the world. In reality, Squaw Valley had little aside from its impressive natural resources to merit hosting the Olympic Games. But the crafty Cushing inspired the state of California to commit enough financial resources to upgrade the landscape as required. With California behind him, Cushing convinced the International Olympic Committee to select Squaw Valley as the site for the 1960 Games. The decision created a surge in public interest for the Sierra Nevada and Lake Tahoe Basin and changed the landscape forever.

Ironically, twice as many visitors come to the region in summer than winter. Warm-weather activities include hiking, mountain biking, and water activities centered around crystal clear Lake Tahoe. Summer and winter, the High Camp cable car departs regularly to climb beyond a striking rock precipice that towers over the valley. In an interesting twist, Squaw Valley's beginner ski slopes are located near the top of the mountain, which affords everyone—no matter what their level of skiing expertise—an excuse to head toward the summit. The mountaintop swimming pool also features a year-round collection of nonskiers who prefer a less aerobic approach to alpine life.

BALBOA BURGER WITH PICKLED ONIONS

A much-loved tradition at Balboa Cafe in San Francisco, the Balboa Burger has now also found its way to the cafe's Squaw Valley outpost, where hungry skiers devour it to fuel their passion on the slopes. What makes this burger so special? In this case, form is everything. Instead of a traditional round patty, the Balboa Burger is torpedo-shaped, to fit into a French baguette. Equally important are Balboa Cafe's classic tangy pickled red onions, served on the side or on the burger.

Pickled onions are easy to make, but the process requires about twenty-four hours of brining. Quite powerful on the palate, a little of these onions goes a long way, but leftovers keep for weeks.

At the cafes, these burgers are typically served with french fries. But in the absence of a commercial fryer, they are equally delicious at home when accompanied by Oven-Roasted Potato "Fries" (page 91) or Skins-On Mashed Potatoes (page 92).

MAKES 4 BURGERS

AND IN YOUR GLASS

GIVEN THE SPICY-SWEET NATURE OF THE ONIONS AND THE TENDENCY OF MOST AMERICANS TO EAT BURGERS WITH KETCHUP AND MUSTARD, IT MAKES SENSE TO LOOK FOR A WINE THAT OFFERS GOOD ACIDITY, FORWARD FRUIT, AND THE FULLNESS FOUND IN MANY RED WINES. ZINFANDEL, GRENACHE, AND SYRAH ALL PAIR WELL WITH THE BALBOA BURGER. SO DO CHILLED DRY ROSÉS, WHICH COOL DOWN THE PALATE AFTER A BITE OF HOT PICKLED ONIONS!

FOR THE PICKLED ONIONS

1 large red onion, thinly sliced	¼ cup kosher or other coarse salt
2 cups Champagne vinegar	1 bay leaf
1 cup water	2 teaspoons red pepper flakes
½ cup sugar	2 whole cloves
2 cloves garlic, peeled	

Put the onion into a medium nonreactive mixing bowl.

In a saucepan, combine the vinegar, water, sugar, garlic, salt, bay leaf, red pepper flakes, and cloves and bring to a boil. Pour the boiling brine over the onion slices, cover the bowl with a plate, and leave at room temperature for 24 hours. (You don't need to refrigerate at this point. The pickling brine creates an unsuitable environment for bacteria.) Leftovers can be stored, refrigerated, in a sealed plastic container for up to several weeks.

continued on page 154

FOR THE BURGERS

2 pounds ground beef

½ teaspoon coarse salt

Freshly ground pepper

1 teaspoon canola oil (optional)

2 fresh baguettes

1 head butter lettuce

1 ripe tomato, sliced

1 dill pickle, thinly sliced lengthwise into 4 slices

Ketchup and Dijon mustard, for serving (optional)

If using, prepare an outdoor grill.

In a large mixing bowl, use your hands to mix the beef, salt, and pepper. Divide the meat into 4 balls and toss each ball back and forth between your hands a few times to eliminate air. Place each beef ball on a cutting board and roll into an oblong shape. Gently flatten the burgers while maintaining their long shape to a thickness of about 1 to 1½ inches. They should resemble the shape of a baguette.

If not using an outdoor grill, spread the oil thinly over the surface of a large, heavy skillet and heat over medium-high heat. When the skillet or grill is hot, cook the burgers for about 5 minutes per side for medium-rare, 7 minutes per side for medium.

Cut the baguettes into lengths comparable to the burgers and slice open lengthwise to serve as a bun. Sandwich each burger inside a baguette. Cut them in half for easier handling at the table.

Set each bunned burger on a plate. Stack a few lettuce leaves next to the burger and top them with a slice of tomato and dill pickle. Place a mound of pickled onions next to the lettuce and tomato. Diners can load up their burgers with the garnish or enjoy them on the side. Ketchup and mustard are optional.

THAI BEEF SALAD

Crunchy snow peas, carrots, and peanuts contrast here with soft papaya and tender tenderloin of beef, all topped with a tangy peanut sauce. Served on a large plate with white rice, this "salad" becomes a main course.

Although there appear to be many steps to this recipe, it is actually quite simple to prepare. First, make your three sauces—the meat marinade, the Thai vinaigrette, and the peanut sauce. Then prepare the rice, meat, and vegetables.

Thai chile sauces and mirin, a sweet rice wine, are found in the Asian foods section of many grocery stores. Fish sauce is an earthy, pungent liquid commonly used in Asian cooking. It will most likely be found on a store shelf near the mirin. Lemongrass is found in many grocery produce sections. If necessary, peel off the outer layer of skin, which might be bruised, before slicing into thin rounds or chopping. No more than one stalk is required. MAKES 4 SERVINGS

AND IN YOUR GLASS

TRY A WINE THAT TYPICALLY SERVES UP HINTS OF THE TROPICS, SUCH AS MANGO-LIKE VIOGNIER OR SAUVIGNON BLANC WITH A HINT OF GOOSEBERRY. A FRUITY CALIFORNIA ROSÉ OR A HIGH-END SAKE WOULD BE EXCELLENT CHOICES AS WELL. DESPITE THE PRESENCE OF BEEF, STAY AWAY FROM RED WINES. THEY WON'T STAND UP WELL TO THE TANGY VINAIGRETTE AND PEANUT SAUCE.

FOR THE MARINADE

½ cup Mae Ploy or any other commercial Thai sweet chile sauce

¼ cup peanut oil

¼ cup canola oil

1 tablespoon chopped fresh ginger

2 cups loosely packed chopped fresh cilantro

In a blender or food processor, pulse all the ingredients to blend. Transfer marinade to a large bowl.

FOR THE VINAIGRETTE

½ cup fresh lime juice

¼ cup diced shallots

1 jalapeño pepper, seeded, stemmed, and minced

¼ cup mirin

3 tablespoons sugar

1 teaspoon chopped fresh ginger

2 tablespoons toasted sesame oil

1½ teaspoons fish sauce

In a small bowl, combine the lime juice with the shallots and jalapeño. Set aside.

In a saucepan, mix the mirin, sugar, and ginger. Bring to a boil and stir occasionally until all the sugar is dissolved, about 2 minutes. Puree in a blender, then pour into the lime juice mixture. Whisk in the sesame oil and fish sauce to blend thoroughly. Set aside.

continued on page 157

FOR THE PEANUT SAUCE

1 tablespoon peanut oil	1 cup canned coconut milk
2 tablespoons chopped lemongrass	¼ cup peanut butter
2 tablespoons diced onion	2 tablespoons soy sauce or tamari
1 tablespoon minced fresh ginger	1 tablespoon dark toasted sesame oil
2 cloves garlic, minced	½ teaspoon fish sauce
¼ cup mirin	

In a saucepan, heat the peanut oil over medium heat until it moves easily in the pan. Add the lemongrass, onion, ginger, and garlic and cook until the onion is translucent, about 3 minutes. Pour the mirin into the pan and break up any bits of garlic or onion that may be stuck to the bottom. Simmer for 2 minutes. Add the coconut milk, peanut butter, soy sauce, sesame oil, and fish sauce and stir until the peanut butter melts and is incorporated into the sauce. Remove from the heat and reserve. Serve warm or at room temperature. (You can save extra sauce in the refrigerator for up to 3 days.)

FOR THE BEEF AND VEGETABLES

1½ pounds beef tenderloin, cut into 1-inch cubes	½ green or moderately ripe papaya, seeded, peeled, and sliced
¼ cup toasted peanuts (page 192)	4 leaves romaine lettuce, sliced in narrow strips
1 carrot, sliced in narrow strips, 2 to 3 inches long	2 cups cooked white rice (page 192), for serving
½ pound snow peas, sliced in narrow, long strips	
1 zucchini, sliced in narrow strips 2 to 3 inches long	

Prepare an outdoor grill or preheat broiler. Soak bamboo skewers in water for 20 minutes.

Toss the meat in the meat marinade and let sit for 5 minutes, tossing once or twice again to coat well. Pack the cubes on the skewers. Broil or grill the meat, turning every 3 or 4 minutes, until the meat is cooked but still pink on the inside. (Be careful not to pick up hot skewers with your bare hands.) Remove the meat from the skewers prior to serving.

While the meat is cooking, pour the Thai vinaigrette into a large salad bowl. Toss the peanuts, carrot, snow peas, zucchini, papaya, and lettuce in the vinaigrette.

Place a pile of grilled meat cubes on 4 dinner plates, flanked on each side by a mound of rice and a mound of tossed salad. Drizzle the peanut sauce over the meat, or serve the sauce on the side.

Rib-Eye Steak with Red Wine Sauce, Salt-Roasted Potatoes, and Warm Blue Lake Bean Salad

If you're looking for a serious meat-and-potatoes fix, you've come to the right recipe. Juicy, tender rib-eye steak is best grilled, seasoned simply with a little salt and pepper. (You can broil with similar results.) The accompanying intensely flavored red wine sauce is used sparingly to bring out the best in the meat.

Surprisingly, burying potatoes in salt doesn't lead to particularly salty spuds. This cooking method results in a mildly salty crust that surrounds a firm yet tender potato marked by a hint of minerality. The potatoes require a couple of hours in the oven, though. Start cooking them well in advance of the meat and beans.

Blue Lake beans are tender, round, stringless "string" beans. They are known to be particularly sweet and juicy, but any fresh string beans will also do nicely here. Prepare them as the steak begins to cook, and serve warm in a side dish. MAKES 4 SERVINGS

AND IN YOUR GLASS

CHOOSE A FULL-BODIED RED TO ACCOMPANY THIS DISH. CABERNET SAUVIGNON, SYRAH, OR ZINFANDEL WOULD ALL SERVE WELL.

FOR THE POTATOES

3 cups kosher or coarse salt

2 pounds medium red-skinned potatoes, scrubbed

2 to 3 tablespoons extra virgin olive oil

Freshly ground pepper

Preheat oven to 350°F.

Place a layer of salt in the bottom of a medium (about 10 inches in diameter) ovenproof pan. Set the potatoes in the salt and cover them with the remaining salt. Bake until tender (when you can insert a fork easily into the potatoes), 1½ to 2 hours. Remove the potatoes from the oven and let cool for a few minutes. Rub excess salt from the skins. Cover to keep warm and set aside. Just prior to serving the steak, quarter the potatoes and gently toss them in a bowl with the olive oil. Serve alongside the steak, seasoned with pepper to taste.

 *continued on page 160*

FOR THE STEAK AND RED WINE SAUCE

2 cups red wine

1½ cups rich veal stock or demi-glace, homemade (pages 196 and 197) or commercial

2 pounds rib-eye steak

Coarse salt and freshly ground pepper

Prepare an outdoor grill or preheat broiler.

Heat 1 cup of the wine in a saucepan over medium-high heat and reduce to about 1 tablespoon, until it almost seems to disappear. Then add the remaining 1 cup of wine and reduce until the wine becomes syrupy. Reduce the heat to medium and add ½ cup of the stock or demi-glace and reduce by half. Add another ½ cup stock and reduce by half, then add the remaining ½ cup stock and reduce until the sauce is smooth and coats the back of a spoon.

While the sauce is reducing, season the steaks with salt and pepper on both sides. Grill or broil the steaks for 8 to 10 minutes per side for medium-rare, depending on the thickness of the steak. Let the steaks rest on a cutting board for 5 minutes, then cut into ¼-inch-thick slices.

FOR THE BEAN SALAD

1 pound Blue Lake or other green beans, stems trimmed

2 tablespoons extra virgin olive oil

2 teaspoons balsamic vinegar

1 teaspoon Dijon mustard

½ teaspoon dried thyme

1 shallot, finely sliced

Coarse salt and freshly ground pepper

Set a steamer basket over 1 inch of water in a large saucepan or fill the pan three-fourths full of lightly salted water. Steam or boil the beans until they are tender but not wilted or faded, 5 to 7 minutes. Transfer to a colander and rinse briefly—about 30 seconds—with cold water to stop them from cooking and to preserve the color. Cover to keep warm.

In a large bowl, whisk together the olive oil, vinegar, mustard, and thyme. Stir in the sliced shallot. Add the beans and toss until they are evenly covered with the vinaigrette. Serve warm, seasoned with salt and pepper to taste.

To serve, arrange slices of steak and some potatoes on 4 dinner plates, and drizzle the steak with the wine sauce. Pass the beans at the table.

Braised Short Ribs Shepherd's Pie

This hearty dish is front-loaded with intensely concentrated flavor. Traditionally, shepherd's pie uses ground meat or stew cuts. But this version features ribs, which are cooked so tender that the meat literally falls off the bone. While slow cooking and the preliminary marinade take time, the dish can be cooked in one pot, with the addition of a saucepan for the wine gravy and another pot for the potatoes. A bit of culinary juggling is involved, but it's well worth it. Short ribs never tasted this good! MAKES 6 SERVINGS

AND IN YOUR GLASS

TRY THIS DISH WITH A
RICHLY STYLED RED WINE
SUCH AS CABERNET
SAUVIGNON, MERLOT,
SYRAH, OR PETITE SIRAH.

4 to 5 pounds beef short ribs, excess fat trimmed

6 cloves garlic, coarsely chopped

1 carrot, coarsely chopped

1 onion, diced

½ teaspoon dried thyme

Coarse salt and freshly ground pepper

1 bottle dry red wine, plus more if necessary (use any moderately priced red)

2 tablespoons canola oil

4 cups chicken stock (page 194) or canned low-sodium chicken or beef broth

Skins-On Mashed Potatoes (page 92)

1 tablespoon unsalted butter

Grated fresh horseradish root or prepared white horseradish, for serving (optional)

Place the ribs in a large, deep nonreactive bowl and add the garlic, carrot, onion, thyme, 2 teaspoons salt, and ½ teaspoon pepper. Pour the wine over all the ingredients to cover. (Depending on the size of your ribs, you may need a little additional wine.) Cover the bowl and refrigerate for 12 to 24 hours.

When the ribs have marinated, remove them from the bowl, season with salt and pepper, and set aside. Strain the liquid from the wine marinade and reserve. Reserve the marinated garlic, carrot, and onion as well.

Preheat oven to 350°F.

In a Dutch oven or large, deep ovenproof pot, heat the canola oil over medium-high heat until it shimmers. Add the ribs and cook, meat side down, until the meat is nicely browned, about 10 minutes. (If you can't fit all the ribs without crowding, brown them in batches.) Flip the ribs to the bony side and cook for 2 more minutes. Remove them from the pot and set aside.

continued on page 162

Add the marinated vegetables to the pot and sauté over medium-high heat, stirring occasionally, for 5 minutes. Add the reserved wine, bring to a boil, then simmer over medium heat until reduced by half, 15 to 20 minutes. Return the ribs to the pot and add the stock to cover the ribs. (If you need a little more liquid, add water.) Bring to a boil, then turn off the heat. Skim off any foam or fat floating on the surface.

Cover the pot, place it in the oven, and bake until the rib meat is very tender, about 2½ hours. While the ribs are in the oven, make the mashed potatoes, cover, and set aside.

Remove the ribs from the pot and set aside. Strain the liquid from the pot into a small saucepan and discard the vegetables. Keep the empty meat pot handy. Leave the oven on.

When the ribs are cool enough to handle, slide the meat off each bone and reserve. Discard the bones. Place the boneless ribs back in the empty meat pot and cover with the mashed potatoes. Cover the pot and bake for 15 minutes.

While the shepherd's pie is baking, bring the sauce to a boil over medium-high heat; reduce until thick and syrupy, about 15 minutes. Reduce the heat to medium and whisk in the butter, stirring occasionally as it melts.

Remove the shepherd's pie from the oven. Serve each portion drizzled with the sauce. Top with the freshly grated horseradish or place a dollop of horseradish on the side, if desired. Garnish with freshly ground pepper to taste.

VENISON RAGOUT WITH POTATO GNOCCHI

Lean venison benefits from a long simmer, which tenderizes the meat and also bathes it in a savory sauce. The meat serves up an enticing hint of gaminess that adds complexity to the ragout. It's tossed with fluffy gnocchi, which are coated in the sauce for an unusual pairing of meat and potatoes. You can order farm-raised venison from most butchers, but if finding it proves to be difficult, try this recipe with lamb. MAKES 6 SERVINGS

AND IN YOUR GLASS

THIS RICH STEW WILL BE ENHANCED BY A FULL-BODIED RED WINE. TRY CABERNET SAUVIGNON, SYRAH, PETITE SIRAH, OR ZINFANDEL. PINOT NOIR AND SANGIOVESE, LIGHTER-STYLED REDS, WOULD ADD AN INTERESTING DIMENSION TO THE MEAL.

3 tablespoons extra virgin olive oil

1 large onion, diced

2 cloves garlic, minced

2 pounds boneless venison loin or shoulder, cut into 1½-inch cubes

1 cup dry red wine

1 large carrot, sliced into thin rounds

¼ cup fresh thyme leaves

1 bay leaf

1½ teaspoons coarse salt

Freshly ground pepper

2 tablespoons tomato paste

2 pounds tomatoes, peeled and diced

2 cups chicken stock (page 194) or canned, low-sodium chicken broth

Gnocchi, homemade (page 94; you don't need the pesto), or 2 pounds commercial

In a large, deep skillet or pot, heat the olive oil over medium-high heat until it shimmers. Add the onion and garlic and sauté until the onion becomes translucent, about 3 minutes, stirring occasionally to prevent the garlic from burning. Stir in the venison and cook until the meat has browned, about 5 minutes, stirring occasionally. Add the wine, carrot, thyme, bay leaf, salt, and pepper to taste. Bring the wine to a boil, reduce the heat, and simmer for 5 minutes.

Place the tomato paste in a small bowl. Take 4 to 5 tablespoons of liquid from the skillet and stir it into the paste. Add the dissolved paste, tomatoes, and chicken stock to the skillet and bring to a boil. Reduce the heat to low, cover, and simmer for 45 minutes. Uncover the pot, increase the heat to medium-high, and cook for 15 to 20 more minutes to thicken the sauce.

In a large pot of boiling water, cook all the gnocchi at once, removing them from the water with a slotted spoon as they rise to the surface. Set them in a colander to drain.

Transfer the gnocchi to a large bowl. Add the venison ragout and stir gently. Serve with freshly ground pepper to taste.

Lamb Chops with Olive Tapenade and Quinoa Tabouli

Gamey lamb chops are a natural partner for the earthy, briny Provençal olive sauce known as *tapenade*. Quinoa tabouli, a starch and salad in one, serves as an excellent accompaniment. MAKES 4 SERVINGS

AND IN YOUR GLASS

LAMB AND SYRAH ARE TRADITIONAL FOOD AND WINE PARTNERS. CABERNET SAUVIGNON CAN ALSO STAND UP TO THIS POWERFULLY FLAVORED MEAT. THE TAPENADE IS A BIT OF A WILD CARD, WITH ITS SALTY, SEA-LIKE QUALITIES COMING FROM THE ANCHOVIES. WITH THIS IN MIND, DRY ROSÉ— SPORTING BRIGHT ACIDITY FOR BALANCE—MIGHT ALSO BE A GOOD SELECTION FOR YOUR WINEGLASS.

FOR THE TAPENADE

1 cup pitted black olives, such as kalamata

⅓ cup extra virgin olive oil

5 cloves garlic confit (page 190)

3 anchovy fillets

1 tablespoon capers

Juice of ½ lemon

¼ teaspoon paprika

In a blender or food processor, pulse all of the ingredients to blend. The tapenade should retain a somewhat coarse, firm consistency. Do not puree.

FOR THE TABOULI

2 cups vegetable stock (page 195) or canned low-sodium vegetable broth

1 cup quinoa (see note on page 166)

1 medium cucumber, peeled and diced

2 medium tomatoes, diced

Leaves from 10 sprigs parsley, chopped

Leaves from 4 or 5 mint sprigs, chopped

½ cup extra virgin olive oil

Juice of ½ lemon

Coarse salt and freshly ground pepper

In a medium pot or saucepan, bring the vegetable stock to a boil. Stir in the quinoa, reduce the heat to simmer, cover, and cook until all the liquid has been absorbed, 10 to 15 minutes.

In a large mixing bowl, combine the cooked quinoa with the cucumber, tomatoes, parsley, mint, olive oil, and lemon juice. Season with salt and pepper. Cover to keep warm.

continued on page 166

FOR THE LAMB

8 lamb loin chops	1 tablespoon extra virgin olive oil
Coarse salt and freshly ground pepper	1 tablespoon dried rosemary, crumbled

Prepare an outdoor grill or preheat broiler.

Season the lamb chops lightly with salt and pepper. Rub the chops with the olive oil and sprinkle evenly with the rosemary.

Grill or broil the chops, turning once, until nicely browned on the outside but still pink inside, 5 to 7 minutes per side.

Transfer to dinner plates, 2 chops per serving, and top each chop with a dollop of the tapenade. Serve with a mound of quinoa tabouli on the side.

Note: Once a staple of the ancient Incas, small-grained quinoa makes a fine alternative to cracked wheat or bulgur, more commonly used in tabouli. Quinoa can be found in most specialty food shops and in an increasing number of supermarkets as well.

Lamb Shanks in Red Wine with Pomegranate/Mint Gremolata, Green Beans, and Chickpeas

The elegant, fresh mint sauce that garnishes these rustic lamb shanks is a variation of the traditional mix of parsley, garlic, and lemon peel known as *gremolata*, which is often added to stews and other dishes such as osso buco. In this version, mint is paired with a single tablespoon of intense pomegranate molasses. The sauce provides just a hint of herbal sweetness and highlights the lamb's earthy richness.

Make the gremolata and the dressing for the beans, both of which require only a short time to prepare, while the lamb is in the oven. The green beans are quick-cooking, of course, and can be prepared immediately prior to serving the meat. MAKES 4 SERVINGS

FOR THE LAMB SHANKS

4 lamb shanks, cracked (see note on page 169)

Coarse salt and freshly ground pepper

4 tablespoons extra virgin olive oil

10 cloves garlic, coarsely chopped

1 onion, coarsely chopped

1 carrot, coarsely chopped

2 ribs celery, coarsely chopped

2 bay leaves

2 sprigs rosemary

4 to 5 cups red wine

Preheat oven to 375°F.

Trim excess fat from the lamb shanks and sprinkle them with salt and pepper. In a Dutch oven or large, deep ovenproof pot, heat 2 tablespoons of the olive oil over high heat until it shimmers. Sear the lamb shanks on all sides, 2 to 3 minutes per side. Remove them from the pot and set aside.

Reduce the heat to medium and add the remaining 2 tablespoons oil. Add the garlic, onion, carrot, celery, bay leaves, and rosemary and cook, stirring occasionally, until the onion becomes translucent, about 10 minutes. Add 4 cups of red wine, stirring to dissolve any solids that may have stuck to the bottom of the pot. Increase the heat to high and return the shanks to the pot. Add more wine if necessary; the shanks should be barely covered. When the wine begins to boil, cover the pot and place it in the oven. Braise until the lamb shanks are very tender, 2 to 2½ hours.

continued on page 169

FOR THE GREMOLATA

3 cloves garlic confit (page 190)

Leaves from 10 to 12 sprigs mint

Leaves from 4 sprigs flat-leaf parsley

½ cup extra virgin olive oil

1 tablespoon pomegranate molasses (see note below)

Place all the ingredients in a blender and pulse to blend well. Reserve at room temperature until ready to use.

FOR THE GREEN BEANS AND CHICKPEAS

Leaves from 5 sprigs mint

1 teaspoon minced fresh ginger

1 tablespoon garlic oil (from the garlic confit, page 190)

3 tablespoons extra virgin olive oil

Coarse salt

½ pound green beans, trimmed

1 cup canned chickpeas, rinsed and drained

In a blender, puree the mint, ginger, garlic oil, and olive oil. Season with a pinch of salt. Set aside.

Set a steamer basket over 1 inch of water in a large saucepan or fill the pan three-fourths full of water. Steam or boil the green beans until they are tender-crisp, about 5 minutes. Transfer to a colander and rinse with cold water to cool and set the color. Shake off excess water.

In a large saucepan, heat the mint/ginger puree over medium heat. Add the green beans and chickpeas. Toss them to coat with the oil and reheat.

Divide the green beans and chickpeas evenly among 4 dinner plates. Lay a lamb shank on top of the beans and top each shank with a spoonful or two of the gremolata. Spoon pan juices from the cooked lamb onto each plate around the edge of the beans and chickpeas. Garnish with pomegranate seeds, if you wish.

Notes: Ask your butcher to "crack" the lamb shanks, which allows for a shorter cooking time.

Pomegranate molasses can be found in specialty stores and on the syrup shelf of many supermarkets.

DESSERT

At its best, dessert highlights a fine dining experience with gentle finality. It shouldn't overwhelm; this final course should, instead, grace the palate with pleasure. The Plump-Jack chefs all share this philosophy, which is easily translated to the home. Sometimes a light-textured touch of sweetness is all that's required, as in the Navel Orange Soufflé featured on page 174. At the other end of the spectrum lies the rich Flourless Hazelnut/Almond Chocolate Cake (page 186). And in between are desserts such as Maple Crème Brûlée (page 182) and—assuming you eat only one or two—Chocolate/Cognac Truffles (page 172).

Sweet dessert wines complement many desserts. These late-harvest wines are often made with grapes that have been allowed to reach an ultra-ripe level of maturity, which produces extra sugar in the juice. Not all of this sugar is fermented, leaving varying levels of sweetness in the finished wine.

In California, late-harvest wines are made from both red and white grapes. It's important to remember that white dessert wines maintain a level of delicacy that may be overwhelmed by heavier desserts, particularly those made with chocolate. Red dessert wines, which may also include fortified wines made in the style of Port, are decidedly more chocolate-friendly.

Another way to enjoy a dessert wine is after dessert has been eaten. The temptation of tucking into that second piece of cake is severely reduced when a soothing, sweet after-dinner drink waits in the wings!

CHOCOLATE/COGNAC TRUFFLES

With just a hint of Cognac on the finish, these lush chocolate morsels make a perfect mealtime finale. Really fine chocolate is blessed with silky cocoa crystals that you'll want to preserve by gently melting with cream that is not ultra-hot but just shy of boiling. Remember that the quality of your truffles will depend on the quality of the chocolate you use. Try using one of the many "boutique" brands in the marketplace today that produce intensely flavored bittersweet chocolate with a very low cocoa-butter content. MAKES ABOUT 25 TRUFFLES

AND IN YOUR GLASS

CHOCOLATE AND DRY WINE DON'T REALLY MIX BECAUSE THE SWEETNESS OF THE CHOCOLATE TENDS TO MAKE A DRY WINE TASTE BITTER. HOWEVER, SWEET RED WINES MADE IN THE FULL-BODIED STYLE OF PORT OFFER THE KIND OF BODY AND RICHNESS THAT PAIR EASILY WITH THESE CHOCOLATE TRUFFLES. A BRANDY WOULD ALSO MAKE A FINE CHOICE.

8 ounces bittersweet chocolate, finely chopped

1 cup heavy cream

1 tablespoon Cognac or other brandy

5 tablespoons cold unsalted butter, cut into pieces

Confectioners' sugar, for dusting

½ cup cocoa powder

Place the chopped chocolate in a large bowl. In a saucepan, heat the cream over medium heat until steam begins to rise and you see just a hint of tiny bubbles at the edge of the liquid. (Do not boil, however.) Immediately pour over the chocolate. Whisk gently until the chocolate has completely melted. Whisk in the brandy. Let sit to cool slightly, about 5 minutes. Add the butter pieces and blend with a whisk. Cover and refrigerate until firm to the touch, at least 2 or 3 hours.

Dust a 1-inch ice-cream scoop or a melon baller with confectioners' sugar to prevent sticking and scoop out the truffle mix. Dust your hands with more sugar to prevent sticking and roll the scoops into balls. Place them on a pie pan and freeze for 2 hours.

Pour the cocoa powder into a bowl. Remove the truffles from the freezer and gently roll them in the cocoa powder until coated evenly. Store in an airtight container in the refrigerator for up to 1 week. Take the truffles out of the refrigerator 30 minutes before serving.

Navel Orange Soufflé

The PlumpJack chefs often use red-hued blood oranges when they are in season instead of navel oranges. These change the color of this delicate soufflé from a subtle light orange to pink. Either way, this soufflé serves up the perfect counterpoint to an otherwise filling repast. With tangy orange essence suspended in weightless egg whites, the dish has an almost ethereal quality.

Airy soufflés are best when served immediately after baking. For this dessert soufflé, it pays to make the orange/sugar base as much as a day or two in advance. This way, you can simply whip up the egg whites, fold in the orange base, and bake—all within about 20 minutes of your main dinner course. (Leftover soufflé can be refrigerated and later heated up in a microwave oven. It's not quite as good as the freshly baked version, but it still has merit.) MAKES 8 SERVINGS

AND IN YOUR GLASS

THOSE WHO ENJOY DESSERT WINES MIGHT PAIR THIS DISH WITH A LATE-HARVEST MOSCATO—OR MUSCAT—WINE, REDOLENT OF ORANGE ZEST AND SPICE ON THE FINISH.

2 medium navel oranges

1 cup granulated sugar, plus more for dusting

⅓ cup cornstarch

3 tablespoons water

10 large egg whites

1 teaspoon cream of tartar

Confectioners' sugar, for dusting

Cut the rind and pith from the oranges. Halve the oranges across the equator and take out the seeds, then cut them into chunks and put them in a blender or food processor. Pulse the oranges until they are reduced to a smooth puree.

Pour the puree into a small saucepan, stir in the 1 cup granulated sugar, and bring to a boil over medium heat, stirring occasionally to prevent sticking. While the orange/sugar mixture is heating up, place the cornstarch in a bowl and add the water. Stir with a small wooden spoon until it becomes smooth. Stir the cornstarch slurry into the orange/sugar mixture. When it begins to boil, reduce the heat and simmer for 5 minutes. Transfer to a nonreactive bowl and let cool to room temperature. (Or store in the refrigerator for up to 2 days, but remember to bring it to room temperature before folding into the egg whites; see below).

Preheat oven to 375°F. Butter eight 6-ounce ramekins and dust them with granulated sugar.

Place the egg whites and cream of tartar in a large bowl. Using an electric mixer, whip the egg whites at high speed until they form stiff peaks. Gently fold in the orange-based mixture with a wooden spoon or rubber spatula until it is thoroughly incorporated into the egg whites.

Fill each ramekin to the top with the soufflé mixture and smooth flat with a rubber spatula. Place the ramekins on a baking sheet and set them on the top rack in the oven. Bake for 10 to 15 minutes, until the soufflés have risen about ½ inch above the ramekins and are golden brown on top. Remove from the oven and dust with confectioners' sugar. Serve immediately.

Nectarine and Blackberry Cobbler

There are more than grapes growing in the Napa Valley. Nectarine trees grace the gardens of many locals, while wild blackberry bushes line back roads and trails from San Francisco up through the valley to points farther north. The produce department of your local supermarket should also be able to satisfy any cravings you may have for the fresh ripe fruit used here. Tuck into this tangy tart for an exquisite taste of summer. Perfect for picnics or potlucks. MAKES 8 SERVINGS

FOR THE FILLING

8 ripe nectarines, pits removed but skin intact, cut into 1-inch chunks

2 baskets blackberries (6 ounces each)

1 cup sugar

2 tablespoons all-purpose flour

1 tablespoon unsalted butter, melted

In a large bowl, combine the nectarine pieces, blackberries, sugar, flour, and melted butter. Using a large spoon, gently mix, then pour into a 9-by-13-inch baking dish. Set aside.

FOR THE TOPPING

2 cups all-purpose flour, plus more as needed

2 tablespoons sugar

2 teaspoons baking powder

½ teaspoon coarse salt

1 cup heavy cream

1 large egg, beaten

Whipped cream (page 201; optional)

Vanilla ice cream (optional)

AND IN YOUR GLASS
A CLASSIC AMERICAN
DESSERT DESERVES A
CLASSIC AMERICAN CUP
OF COFFEE.

Preheat oven to 375°F.

In a large bowl, combine the 2 cups flour, sugar, baking powder, and salt and whisk to mix thoroughly. Stir in the cream to begin making your dough. In the bowl, push down on the dough with the heel of your hand and spread it forward at bit. Fold it back onto itself and repeat the spreading and folding several times, lightly flouring your hands, if necessary, to prevent the dough from sticking. When the dough is smooth and malleable, form it into a large ball. Turn the dough out onto a lightly floured surface and roll it to a size that will cover a 9-by-13-inch baking dish.

Cover the fruit mixture with the rolled-out cobbler topping. Using a fork, poke holes evenly in the top of the dough at 3-inch intervals. Glaze the top of the cobbler with the beaten egg.

Set the cobbler in the oven and bake until the crust is golden brown, 35 to 45 minutes. Cut into individual portions and serve warm or at room temperature. If desired, serve with whipped cream or vanilla ice cream.

Orange/Olive Oil Cake

This fruity cake offers an unusual blend of sweet and bitter flavors. Olive oil contributes an exotic edge while keeping the cake quite soft and moist. The soft crumb provides contrast to crunchy almonds, while tangy citrus adds high notes. MAKES 2 LOAVES, EACH 9 BY 5 INCHES

2 navel oranges	2 teaspoons baking powder
1 lemon	½ teaspoon baking soda
4 large eggs	1 cup toasted almonds (page 192), chopped
1½ cups sugar	
½ teaspoon coarse salt	⅔ cup extra virgin olive oil, plus more for the pans
1 cup all-purpose flour	

AND IN YOUR GLASS

TRY THIS CAKE WITH A DESSERT WINE SUCH AS LATE-HARVEST MUSCAT OR SAUVIGNON BLANC. THOSE WHO LIKE SOMETHING SWEET IN THE MORNING MIGHT FIND THIS MOIST CAKE PAIRS WELL WITH CAPPUCCINO, TOO.

Preheat oven to 350°F. Oil two 9-by-5-inch loaf pans with olive oil.

Use a vegetable peeler to remove the zest from 1 of the oranges and the lemon. In a small saucepan, blanch the zests in boiling water for 30 seconds. Let cool, chop fine, and reserve. Peel the remaining orange and discard the skin. Remove as much white pith as you can from both oranges and the lemon. If you have good knife skills, slice each orange segment free from its membrane and chop the segments into small pieces. Otherwise, simply separate the orange segments and chop them up. Do the same for the lemon. Remove as much pithy membrane and seeds as you can. Reserve along with the chopped orange segments.

In a large bowl, whisk the eggs, sugar, and salt until the eggs are pale and doubled in volume, about 5 minutes. In another bowl, whisk together the flour, baking powder, and baking soda. Mix in the almonds. Stir the dry mixture into the egg batter and blend thoroughly. Add the chopped citrus zests and segments and stir well. Stir in the ⅔ cup olive oil until blended evenly.

Evenly divide the cake mix between the 2 loaf pans and bake for 35 to 40 minutes, or until the cakes are firm and a toothpick inserted comes out dry. Cool on a rack for 10 minutes, then turn out and cool completely.

Napa Valley

History among the Vines

After crossing the windswept Golden Gate Bridge, travelers leaving San Francisco drive north to the wine country. Within an hour, they find themselves touring the narrow roads that traverse Napa Valley's vine-studded hillsides. The first stop is the Carneros region. Here at the southern edge of the valley, cool bay breezes caress vines that produce some of the most sought-after Pinot Noir and Chardonnay in the New World.

Wine, of course, is the lifeblood of the area. As early as 1830, grapes were planted on the neighboring Sonoma side of the Carneros region by Mexico's General Mariano Guadalupe Vallejo. Twenty years later, California had achieved statehood, and a new breed of wine pioneers were moving into the Napa Valley. They included men like George Yount, who had worked with Vallejo and to whom Vallejo had awarded a Napa Valley land grant in 1836. Yount planted Napa Valley's first vineyard in 1838 on the property that eventually grew into the town of Yountville.

In the 1850s, George Belden Crane established some of the first vineyards in St. Helena, some ten miles north of where Yount was living. And by 1879, Finnish sea captain Gustav Niebaum had established the famed Inglenook winery on a vineyard first planted by George Yount's son-in-law. Niebaum's property is now owned by vintner/filmmaker Francis Ford Coppola, who has renamed his winery Rubicon Estate.

Before the end of the nineteenth century, some 150 wineries had been built on Napa Valley's rocky soil. Included among them was the winery now called PlumpJack. In those early days, American wines were appreciated in both the New and Old Worlds, where they garnered praise in competitions against the French and Germans, who dominated the market at the time.

Unfortunately, the vine louse known as *phylloxera* severely damaged all of California's vineyards and shot down America's rising wine star. *Phylloxera* was ultimately defeated and the vineyards recovered, but in 1920 America's winemakers were faced with Prohibition, which outlawed the production of most commercial wines. It would be another generation before Napa Valley vintners and the California wine industry were back on track.

Today, some 400 wineries are nestled among Napa Valley's extensive vineyards. The days of Prohibition are long forgotten, and a new age of fine winemaking has clearly demonstrated that the region's former glory was not a passing one.

Maple Crème Brûlée

MAPLE CRÈME BRÛLÉE This is crème brûlée with a maple twist. It's easy to make and delivers mounds of creamy sweet pleasure, highlighted by hints of vanilla. A crunchy, caramelized top offers a pleasing textural counterpoint.

Most home cooks don't have a blowtorch handy, but a standard oven broiler does just fine to caramelize the sugar on top. Keep the oven door open a bit to watch, however. The melting sugar can quickly change from golden perfection to dark black if you are not paying attention. MAKES 6 SERVINGS

3 cups heavy cream

1 cup maple syrup

1 vanilla bean, scraped (page 201), or
1 teaspoon vanilla extract

5 large egg yolks

1 large egg white

½ cup sugar

Fresh raspberries or other seasonal berry (optional)

AND IN YOUR GLASS

WHILE THIS DESSERT IS PERFECTLY SELF-SUFFICIENT AND DELICIOUS ON ITS OWN, A SPICY, SWEET RIESLING OR GEWÜRZTRAMINER MIGHT ADD TO YOUR ENJOYMENT.

Preheat oven to 350°F.

In a saucepan, heat the cream, maple syrup, and vanilla bean over medium heat until steam begins to rise. Do not boil. Remove from the heat and set aside.

In a mixing bowl, gently stir the egg yolks and egg white to blend evenly. If you are using the vanilla bean, remove it from the cream and discard. If you are using extract, stir it in now. Slowly pour the eggs into the cream and maple syrup mixture, stopping to stir gently 3 or 4 times. Set the warm custard pan in an ice-water bath to cool for 10 minutes. Stir gently after 5 minutes to facilitate cooling.

Pour the cooled custard into six 6-ounce ramekins. Place the ramekins in a shallow hot-water bath and bake until the custard is firm, about 35 minutes. Remove the ramekins from the water bath and let sit at room temperature for up to 2 hours, or let cool to room temperature and then refrigerate for up to 8 hours.

When you are ready to serve, heat the broiler. Transfer the ramekins to a baking sheet and sprinkle each with the sugar, dividing it evenly. Place the ramekins under the broiler, lining them up directly under the flame or heat source. Remove from the heat when the crème brûlée tops are golden brown. Garnish with raspberries, if desired.

PEANUT BUTTER COOKIES These light-textured cookies are a favorite with both grown-ups and kids at the Balboa Cafe. MAKES ABOUT 30 COOKIES

1¼ cups all-purpose flour	1½ cups granulated sugar
1 teaspoon baking powder	½ cup packed brown sugar
¼ teaspoon coarse salt	1 cup unsalted creamy peanut butter
8 tablespoons (1 stick) unsalted butter, at room temperature	1 large egg, lightly beaten

Preheat oven to 350°F.

In a small bowl, whisk together the flour, baking powder, and salt. Set aside.

In a large bowl, use an electric mixer at medium speed to cream the butter with ½ cup of the granulated sugar, the brown sugar, and the peanut butter until smooth. Scrape the sides of the bowl with a rubber spatula to make sure all the butter is incorporated. Add the egg to the peanut butter mixture. Beat with the mixer for another 30 to 45 seconds. Add the flour mixture and continue to mix until the dough is crumbly, another 30 to 45 seconds.

Pour the remaining 1 cup granulated sugar into a bowl.

Use a teaspoon to gather the dough into rough balls about 1½ inches in diameter. Round them out in the palm of your hand and roll them lightly in the sugar, then place the sugared balls on a nonstick cookie sheet. Use a fork to gently flatten the balls to about ¼ inch thick, with a crisscross design on the tops.

Bake until slightly brown, 10 to 15 minutes. Remove the cookies from the oven and let sit for 1 minute to firm up. Transfer the cookies to wire racks and let cool.

AND IN YOUR GLASS

GREAT WITH A GLASS OF MILK, THESE COOKIES ARE EVEN BETTER WITH ESPRESSO OR CAPPUCCINO AT THE END OF A MEAL.

BANANAS FOSTER BRIOCHE PUDDING This satisfying dessert is
inspired by the famous New Orleans specialty that is part dessert, part showmanship.
Typically, the preparation involves flaming rum and access to a nearby fire
extinguisher. In the interest of preserving your home, we've eliminated the fireworks.
The finished dessert is light on the palate yet brimming with banana and rum flavors.

Sweet, buttery brioche makes a fabulous addition to bread pudding. Look for
brioche loaves at most bakeries and specialty grocery stores. You can use any shape
loaf, since you'll be cutting the bread into small cubes. MAKES 6 SERVINGS

AND IN YOUR GLASS

WITH THE RUM IN THE

PUDDING, THIS DESSERT

PAIRS NICELY WITH

AMERICAN COFFEE OR

ESPRESSO.

2 brioche loaves (about 16 ounces each), unsliced but with ends removed

2 cups heavy cream

1 cup half-and-half

1 whole vanilla bean, split and scraped (see page 201), or 1 teaspoon vanilla extract

½ teaspoon ground cinnamon

2 large eggs, lightly beaten

8 tablespoons (1 stick) unsalted butter

½ cup brown sugar

½ cup granulated sugar

3 ripe bananas, mashed

½ cup dark rum

1½ to 2 cups whipped cream (page 201)

Preheat oven to 300°F.

Cut the brioche loaves into enough 1-inch-square croutons to measure 6 cups. Place the croutons on a flat baking pan or cookie sheet and bake until golden brown, about 15 minutes. Cool the croutons on a rack, then transfer to an 8-inch-square baking pan.

In a medium-large saucepan or pot, heat the cream, half-and-half, and vanilla bean over medium heat until the cream begins to steam. (Do not boil.) Remove from the heat, add the cinnamon, and gently whisk in the eggs. If you are using vanilla extract, stir it in now.

In another medium saucepan, melt the butter over medium heat. Add the brown and granulated sugars and whisk gently until thick and bubbly. Stir in the mashed bananas and mix well. Remove the pan from the heat and whisk in the rum. Return the banana/rum mixture to the heat for 2 more minutes.

If using the vanilla bean, remove it from the custard and discard. Pour the banana mixture into the custard and whisk to blend evenly. Pour over the brioche croutons to cover. Let sit for about 15 minutes, until the liquid is well absorbed by the croutons.

Meanwhile, preheat oven to 350°F.

Bake the pudding in a hot-water bath until firm, about 25 minutes. Let cool and serve slightly warm or at room temperature, graced with a dollop or two of cool, fresh whipped cream.

Flourless Hazelnut/Almond Chocolate Cake

This ultra-rich cake has no frosting—it doesn't need it. But it does have a bit of hazelnut crunch, which provides contrast to the smooth, silky chocolate. Homemade whipped cream (page 201) serves as a cool, refreshing complement to this eminently satisfying dessert.

The recipe calls for a springform pan, which is easiest to remove from the still-warm cake. But a traditional 9-inch baking pan will also work here. Just make sure you let the cake cool sufficiently before removing it from the pan. MAKES 8 TO 10 SERVINGS

8 ounces bittersweet chocolate, coarsely chopped	¾ cup plus 5 tablespoons granulated sugar
2 ounces unsweetened chocolate, coarsely chopped	⅓ cup almond paste
4 ounces hazelnuts, toasted (page 192)	6 large eggs, separated
5 tablespoons confectioners' sugar	2 teaspoons espresso or very strong coffee, cooled
¼ cup cocoa powder	2 teaspoons vanilla extract
12 tablespoons (1½ sticks) unsalted butter, at room temperature, plus more for the pans	1½ to 2 cups whipped cream (page 201)

Preheat oven to 325°F. Butter the bottom and sides of a 9-inch traditional round or springform cake pan. Dust the pan with flour and tap out any excess.

Combine the bittersweet and unsweetened chocolate in a bowl set over a pot of simmering water and melt, stirring occasionally until smooth. Remove from the heat and cover to keep warm.

In a food processor, pulse the hazelnuts, 3 tablespoons of the confectioners' sugar, and the cocoa until they form a coarse powder.

In a medium bowl, use a mixer to beat together the ¾ cup butter and ¾ cup granulated sugar until the mixture is light and fluffy. Beat in the almond paste, occasionally scraping down the sides of the bowl with a rubber spatula, until smooth. Then beat in the egg yolks, espresso, vanilla extract, and the melted chocolate. Fold in the hazelnut mixture with the rubber spatula.

In a separate mixing bowl, use an electric mixer to beat the egg whites until they are foamy. Gradually add the 5 tablespoons granulated sugar and continue beating until stiff peaks form. Using the rubber spatula, gently fold the egg white mixture into the chocolate cake batter.

Pour the batter into the cake pan. Bake until a fork or toothpick inserted into the center comes out dry, about 50 minutes. Let cool for 1 hour before removing the cake from the pan. (If not using a springform pan, invert the cake onto a serving plate and gently tap the bottom of the pan to release it.) Using a fine-mesh sieve, dust the top of the cake with the remaining 2 tablespoons confectioners' sugar. Top individual servings with a dollop of whipped cream.

Basics

The basic preparations highlighted in this chapter can be applied to many of the recipes in this book as well as numerous other dishes in your culinary repertoire. Stocks, beans, and rice, for example, are food foundations that span the cooking traditions of most cultures. And they serve as culinary anchors for both chefs and home cooks.

A fair number of dishes featured in this book require basic stocks, which you can make easily from scratch. In most recipes, we've suggested a commercial substitute as an option. These ready-made kitchen helpers can be quite acceptable in terms of quality, as long as you steer clear of overly salted or otherwise processed products. Still, there is something very satisfying about using a homemade stock or other culinary building block, and we recommend employing them whenever possible.

Some items featured in this section might not be considered staples by everyone, but they are staples in the PlumpJack kitchens and serve as key components for a number of recipes found in these pages. An example would be garlic confit (page 190), made from slow-cooked garlic cloves. This simple preparation yields a luscious, mellow clove and creates a wonderful garlic-infused olive oil as a by-product. Roasted garlic (page 191) has similar attributes but different applications. Once you have begun to use them, these preparations may become basics for you as well.

Use the following recipes and tips for a multitude of culinary requirements. They will serve you well.

GARLIC CONFIT Garlic that is slow-cooked in olive oil adds an earthy, sweet quality to a sauce or dish, since the gentle cooking intensifies flavor while reducing bitterness. Garlic confit is an essential ingredient for a number of recipes in this book, but it has other uses, too. Spread it on crusty country bread for a snack, accompanied by any hearty red wine, and use the oil for a garnish or for cooking other dishes.

10 to 15 medium to large cloves garlic, peeled

2 cups extra virgin olive oil (or oil to cover)

Put the garlic in a small to medium saucepan and pour in enough olive oil to cover. Heat over medium heat until the oil begins to bubble around the garlic. Reduce the heat to low and cook for 30 minutes.

The garlic and oil will keep in a covered container for up to 2 weeks.

ROASTED GARLIC Roasted garlic makes a fine topping for pizza or a garnish for any number of roasted meats, poultry, or fish. Mixed into mashed potatoes, it adds an earthy zing. As a component in our Caesar Salad dressing (page 51), roasted garlic adds a subtly rich sweetness and a layer of added complexity. And it's delicious squeezed out of its peel and slathered on bread or toast.

Fortunately, roasting garlic may be one of the simplest of all culinary activities. If you want, prepare a bigger batch so you'll have it on hand.

1 bulb garlic	1 teaspoon extra virgin olive oil

Preheat oven to 400°F.

Halve the garlic bulb as you would a grapefruit, so that each clove in the bulb is divided in half. Wrap each half in aluminum foil but leave the tops open. Drizzle the olive oil over the exposed garlic and place the bulb halves in the oven. Roast until the tops are golden and the garlic flesh is tender, 45 to 50 minutes. Squeeze the soft garlic out of the skins as needed.

Roasted garlic will keep, wrapped in foil, in the refrigerator for up to 1 week.

Basic Rice (White and Brown) Follow this recipe to make rice that yields tender grains eminently suited to soaking up sauces and juices. MAKES 2 CUPS, OR 4 SIDE DISH SERVINGS

2 cups water, chicken stock (page 194), or canned low-sodium chicken broth

½ teaspoon coarse salt

1 cup white or brown, long- or short-grain rice

In a medium saucepan, bring the water to a boil and add the salt. Stir in the rice and return to a boil. Reduce the heat to low, cover, and cook until all the water has been absorbed, 20 minutes for white rice, 30 to 40 minutes for brown rice.

TOASTING NUTS AND SEEDS

Toasting nuts and seeds highlights their aromatics and also lends a bit of crunchiness to their texture. It is an extremely easy technique that requires nothing more than a sauté pan or small skillet and some minimal focus on the part of the cook. Just be careful not to let your nuts or seeds burn!

In a sauté pan over medium heat, toast seeds or nuts, stirring fairly constantly, until fragrant, 3 to 4 minutes. Larger nuts, such as hazelnuts or almonds, may require more time, 8 to 10 minutes.

FISH STOCK Fish stock can be made with little more than leftover bones, which your fishmonger will gladly give away. The resulting stock delivers a subtly refined base for a number of recipes used in this book, most notably Pan-Roasted Monkfish with Basmati Rice and Coriander Broth (page 121). Fish heads are often used in stock but are not required. The gills may contribute bitterness and should be removed with scissors or a sharp knife. MAKES ABOUT 1 QUART

2 tablespoons extra virgin olive oil

1 onion, coarsely chopped

3 ribs celery, coarsely chopped

1 leek, white part only, cleaned and coarsely chopped

½ fennel bulb, coarsely chopped (optional)

2 pounds fish bones

6 cups water

½ teaspoon dried thyme, 1 bay leaf, and 4 sprigs parsley, all tied in cheesecloth for a bouquet garni

In a medium or large skillet or sauté pan, heat the olive oil over medium heat until it moves easily in the pan. Stir in the onion, celery, leek, and fennel to coat evenly with the oil. Cover and cook for about 15 minutes. Do not brown.

Meanwhile, cut the bones into 4- to 6-inch pieces, rinse them well, and put them in a large pot. Add the water and bring to a boil. Skim off any foam, then reduce the heat to low. Add the bouquet garni and the cooked vegetables. Gently simmer for 30 to 45 minutes. Strain through a fine-mesh sieve and let cool. Discard all solids.

Cover and refrigerate for up to 3 days or freeze for up to 3 months.

CHICKEN STOCK

Chicken stock is not quite like a soup. It's lacking in solids and may not have the intensity of a great chicken soup broth. But it is extremely effective as a cooking liquid that ultimately adds more flavor to a dish than water. Braised meats, rice, soups, and gravy, for example, can all benefit from the use of chicken stock.

You have a lot of options for the base of your stock: the carcass and leftover meat from roast chicken, chicken parts such as backs and necks, or a whole fresh chicken, which may give you a bit more flavor. But leftovers are so practical. Just freeze the carcass and leftovers until you have enough and then make some stock to freeze for future use. MAKES ABOUT 2½ QUARTS

2 to 3 pounds cooked chicken carcass or fresh chicken (see headnote)	1 teaspoon coarse salt
1 onion, coarsely chopped	½ teaspoon dried thyme
1 large carrot, coarsely chopped	1 bay leaf
4 cloves garlic	3 quarts water

In a large pot, combine all the ingredients and bring to a boil. Reduce the heat to low and gently simmer, uncovered, for 1½ hours, skimming off any foam that may collect on the surface. Remove from the heat and strain through a fine-mesh sieve into a clean container.

Discard the solids and let the stock cool. Cover and refrigerate until the fat congeals on the surface. Remove and discard the fat.

Use the stock immediately, or cover and refrigerate for up to 3 days or freeze for up to 3 months.

VEGETABLE STOCK This vegetable stock stands in well for chicken stock, providing a fine base for cooking soups and grains or other dishes that may require stock. Leave the onion skins on to add flavor and color. MAKES ABOUT 6 CUPS

8 cups water

2 medium onions (with skins left on), rinsed, ends trimmed and quartered

4 ribs celery (with leaves intact), cut into 2-inch lengths

3 cloves garlic, peeled and quartered

10 to 15 sprigs parsley

2 bay leaves

2 teaspoons coarse salt

In a large pot, combine all the ingredients and bring to a boil. Reduce the heat to simmer and cook uncovered, skimming off the foam now and then, for 40 minutes. Let cool and strain. Refrigerate for up to 1 week, or freeze for up to 3 months.

VEAL STOCK

Like any stock, veal stock makes an excellent addition to soups and sauces. It can easily stand in for chicken stock, but its unusual intensity makes it particularly useful in creating powerful sauces such as the one used in Ribeye Steak with Red Wine Sauce (page 158). Making veal stock requires a little more effort than most other stocks. Those who don't have time to make veal stock demi-glace (opposite page) from scratch can relax: Many excellent commercial versions are available in most specialty food shops. MAKES ABOUT 2 QUARTS

4 to 5 pounds veal bones, cut into 3-inch pieces	1 carrot, coarsely chopped
2 or 3 veal shanks (about 2 pounds total weight), cut into 3-inch pieces	1 rib celery, coarsely chopped
	10 to 15 black peppercorns
½ cup tomato paste	1 bay leaf
1 bottle red wine	5 quarts water
2 onions, coarsely chopped	3 to 5 sprigs parsley

Preheat oven to 450°F.

Place the bones and shanks in a roasting pan and roast, turning occasionally, until brown on all sides, about 1 hour. Transfer the bones and shanks to a large pot on the stovetop.

Add the tomato paste to the pot and cook over medium-high heat, stirring frequently, until the paste turns a dark reddish brown. Add the wine and stir to dissolve any browned bits from the bottom of the pot. Add the onions, carrot, celery, peppercorns, and bay leaf. Reduce the heat to medium and cook for 10 more minutes. Add the water, bring to a boil, and reduce the heat to simmer. Add the parsley and continue to simmer gently, uncovered, for about 5 hours, skimming off foam occasionally.

Strain the liquid through a sieve and let cool. Discard the solids. Cover and refrigerate for at least 3 hours. Remove and discard the fat that hardens on top.

Cover and refrigerate for up to 3 days or freeze for up to 3 months.

VEAL DEMI-GLACE If you are feeling particularly ambitious, take your veal stock one step farther and reduce it to a thick, concentrated demi-glace. Demi-glace can give many different sauces a particularly silky, smooth, rich texture. It can also be used to bring out an extra hint of intensity in soups or other preparations that require stock. MAKES ABOUT 2 CUPS

Veal stock (opposite page)

Make sure you have removed all the fat from the stock. In a saucepan, bring the stock to a boil and reduce to simmer. Continue to simmer, uncovered, for about 2 hours, until the stock has reduced to about 2 cups. The demi-glace should be thick, rich, and dark brown.

Refrigerate, covered, for up to 3 days or freeze for up to 3 months.

CROUTONS These croutons make a crunchy addition to Caesar Salad (page 51) but are also fun to munch as a snack. MAKES ABOUT 5 CUPS

6 cups day-old bread (preferably baguette or sourdough), cut into ½-inch cubes

4 tablespoons extra virgin olive oil

Pinch of coarse salt

Preheat oven to 350°F.

Place the bread cubes in a large bowl and drizzle the olive oil over them, tossing the cubes so that they are evenly coated. Sprinkle with a pinch of salt and toss again. Transfer the bread cubes to a baking sheet.

Bake, stirring once or twice, until the croutons are crisp, crunchy, and golden brown, about 15 minutes. Let cool. Store in an airtight container for up to 3 days.

PEELING TOMATOES

Professional chefs generally peel tomatoes used in cooking because cooked tomato skins can be papery and unpleasant to chew. However, when simmered in a long-cooking sauce, the skins often break down and are hardly noticeable. Here's an easy way to remove the skins.

With the tip of a paring knife, cut a small, tight circle around the stem end of the tomato and remove it along with the core. Then cut a shallow X in the smooth, blossom end of each tomato.

Blanch the tomatoes in a pot of boiling water or steam them in a steamer for 30 to 40 seconds. Use a slotted spoon to transfer the tomatoes to a bowl of cold water and let cool for a minute. Drain the water and peel off the skins, starting at the X.

BASIC PIZZA DOUGH Pizza dough is easy to make, but—as with any bread—you'll need to allow for rising time. Many recipes call exclusively for all-purpose flour, but all-purpose flour doesn't contain enough gluten, a substance that gives structure to rising dough. High-gluten flour, which is milled from hard wheat, gives fresh country breads as well as pizza crust the chewy texture that is so different from softer cakes and muffins. Too much gluten, however, will yield an overly weighty crust. That's why it makes sense to blend high-gluten flour, often simply labeled "bread flour" or "gluten flour," with all-purpose flour for the most authentic pizza crust.

And what about whole wheat flour? It's true that it contains more nutrients than white flour. But it doesn't rise as easily and makes a heavier crust. The choice is yours. Whatever flour you use, be careful not to roll the crust out too thin, or you may find that your pizza slices fall apart too easily. MAKES ENOUGH FOR 2 PIZZAS, EACH 12 TO 14 INCHES IN DIAMETER

1 envelope (2½ teaspoons) active dry yeast

1¼ cups warm water

½ cup high-gluten flour

2 cups unbleached all-purpose flour, plus more for kneading

2 tablespoons extra virgin olive oil, plus more for the bowls

½ teaspoon coarse salt

In a large bowl, combine the yeast with 1 cup of the warm water. Using a wooden spoon, stir in the high-gluten flour. Add the 2 cups all-purpose flour, the 2 tablespoons olive oil, and the salt. Stir with the wooden spoon until a sticky dough begins to form on the bottom of the bowl. Add the remaining ¼ cup warm water and, with floured hands, shape the dough into a large ball.

Keep your hands floured and continue kneading the dough in the bowl, pushing it down with the heel of your hand, then pulling it together in a mound. Repeat until the dough becomes firm yet elastic, 4 to 5 minutes.

Lightly oil a large clean bowl. Place the dough in the bowl, cover with plastic wrap, and set in a reasonably warm place to rise for about 2 hours, until the dough has doubled in size. (Standard room temperature of 70°F is adequate. Cooler temperatures will slow the rising process.)

After the dough has risen, remove it from the bowl, set it on a floured flat surface, and cut it in half. Using a rolling pin, roll out each half to fit your pizza pans. Raise the edge of the crust with your thumbs to make a rim.

If you are not using the dough immediately, place each half in separate, lightly oiled bowls. Cover the bowls with plastic wrap and refrigerate for up to 8 hours. Or wrap the dough in plastic or place it in a zippered plastic bag and freeze for up to 2 months.

DRIED BEANS With a little advance planning, dried beans are incredibly easy to prepare. An overnight soak is the simplest method. But for those who forget to start early, an alternative exists. Both methods are described below. MAKES ABOUT 5 CUPS

2 cups dried beans   2 teaspoons coarse salt

OVERNIGHT SOAK

Rinse and pick over the beans, then place them in a large bowl with water to cover by 2 inches. Soak overnight.

Drain off the remaining water and transfer the beans to a large pot. Add fresh cold water to cover by 1 to 2 inches and bring to a boil. Add the salt, reduce the heat to simmer, and cook, uncovered, until tender, 45 minutes to 1 hour. (Some beans, such as chickpeas, may take longer—2½ to 3 hours.)

QUICK SOAK

Rinse and pick over the beans. In a large pot, bring 8 cups water and the salt to a boil. Add the beans, cover, and boil for 5 minutes. Remove from the heat and let soak, covered, for 1 to 1½ hours.

Drain the beans in a colander. Return them to the pot, cover with fresh water by 1 to 2 inches, and bring to a boil. Reduce the heat to simmer and cook, uncovered, until tender, 30 to 45 minutes. Drain off any excess water that remains.

REAL WHIPPED CREAM Homemade whipped cream offers diners a versatile foil for many desserts ranging from simple fresh fruits to the Flourless Hazelnut/Almond Chocolate Cake (page 186). And it is deliriously easy to make.

Granulated white sugar is most commonly used, but powdery confectioners' sugar can be substituted, giving the whipped cream a lighter texture. MAKES 1½ TO 2 CUPS

1 cup heavy cream	2 teaspoons sugar

In a deep bowl, combine the cream and sugar. Beat with an electric mixer or a handheld whisk until the cream becomes stiff and peaks form.

SCRAPING A VANILLA BEAN

To prepare a vanilla bean for cooking, lay it flat on a cutting surface. Using a sharp paring knife, slice the bean open lengthwise. Scrape out the paste-like seeds from the interior and discard them. Reserve the bean pod, which has more flavor than the seeds and is easier to use in cooking. By cutting open the pod, more of its surface area is exposed, leading to more effective flavor extraction.

INDEX

Underscored page references indicate boxed text. **Boldfaced** page references indicate photographs.